PAINKILLERS

PAINKILLERS

Real People
Real Pain
Real Jesus

Rev Jacky Connell

ISBN: 1981482040
ISBN 13: 9781981482047

Contents

Pain.

In English, we have only one word for pain. The English word "pain" encompasses all kinds of pain, including physical, emotional, and mental anguish. Physical pain is certainly a serious issue today; people commonly struggle with the pain of conditions like arthritis, fibromyalgia, bad backs, bad knees, and migraines. Even medical treatments can cause pain—like the pain and fatigue associated with chemotherapy and physical rehab after an injury.

But for most people, the physical pain we struggle with pales in comparison to the mental and emotional pain we deal with: Divorce, Abusive childhood, Cheating spouses, Backstabbing friends, and toxic family relationships. Jobs lost and kids gone astray, addictions and loneliness. Then there's the pain of regret: Guilt. Pain over bad decisions and lost opportunities. Everywhere you go, people are in pain.

When you're in pain, getting out of it, or at least numbing it for a while, is all you can think about. But it's important to realize that anytime you're running *away* from something, you are also running *to* something. That's what this book is about.

Where do you run to get away from your pain?

The message that follows in the pages ahead was born during my personal prayer time. When the Lord first spoke to me about developing a teaching series on the subject "Painkillers," I immediately thought what most people think: drugs. Our society is facing the worst drug epidemic in history. Deaths from drug overdoses are up 19 percent in a single year, with deaths from heroin and fentanyl leading the way. The situation is so bad that our government has declared a national public-health emergency.[1]

However, not all people run to substance abuse to escape their pain. There are other things people use to escape their pain, which can be just as devastating. The Lord revealed to me a number of

---

1 http://www.foxnews.com/politics/2017/10/26/trump-to-declare-opioid-public-health-emergency.html.

unhealthy ways in which people try to cope with their pain. Some people escape into isolation. Others run to inappropriate relationships. Still more try to hide in their own spirit of independence. I identified seven different unhealthy painkillers people use to cope with pain.

While I was developing this series of messages, I spoke to many people about these seven painkillers. Most people told me they had used most or all these unhealthy coping mechanisms at one time or another. No one has yet said they've never used one of these to deal with hurt and heartache in his or her life.

It's important to understand that these painkillers are just substitutes. They will never fix your pain; they can only make you think for a while that you're coping with it. In time, these unhealthy painkillers cause you even more pain than whatever hurt and heartache drove you there in the first place.

We will discuss how people get sucked into these unhealthy painkillers and how those pitfalls become strongholds in their lives. We'll talk about the dangers of these unhealthy painkillers, but most importantly, we will talk about God's way of getting us out!

What I want to convey to you is that there is no magic cure for your pain. I don't have a 12-step program or some simplistic A, B, C method to follow for dealing with your pain. I won't tell you, "I understand," because I have never walked through your personal heartache. I can't tell you I know how you feel after losing a child or going through a divorce or having your best friend stab you in the back—those are your pains, and no one else can truly feel that hurt except you. I won't tell you the answer is "Go to church" or "Read your Bible," because many of you have already tried that yet your pain remains. Healing deep emotional pain just isn't that simple or easy.

What I can tell you is that God loves you. He hasn't forgotten you. From the moment the universe was founded and set into motion, He had both a way to get you through your pain and a way to get you away from your unhealthy reactions to pain. Jeremiah 1:5 says, "Before I formed you in the womb I knew you; Before you were born I sanctified you." Whether you're struggling with the loneliness of isolation, the devastation of chemical dependency, or the anguish of insecurity—Jesus is not just a painkiller. He's your Pain Taker.

So thank you for joining me in this journey. I pray that it touches your life in a powerful and meaningful way, as it has already for so many in our congregation at Eden Westside Baptist Church.

*All scripture references are from the New King James version, unless otherwise noted.

1

Isolation

At age thirty-two, Annie had a large family and what she believed to be a strong support system. Suddenly, things started to unravel, quickly and relentlessly. Following the death of her beloved grandparents, Annie went through a divorce, leaving her to raise two children alone. When things got rough financially, her mother abandoned her, telling the family lies and destroying those relationships. After her father was charged with sex crimes against another family member, splitting the family apart even further, Annie essentially lost that side of her family as well.

Annie attempted to find another relationship to replace the void left by her destroyed marriage, but when that didn't work out, she simply decided it was better to just be alone. She moved her children to a new place, avoiding church or any *other social activities, even being a part of her kids' school lives.*

Isolated and alone, Annie replaced healthy social interaction with negative self-talk: "Nobody loves me. I'm all alone. Nobody wants me or ever could want me. Everybody hates me." In this loneliness, worthlessness, and depression, it was all too easy for Satan to lead Annie into deeper problems, like alcohol abuse.

What is isolation? In a word, isolation is separation. You seek to separate yourself from others. When you're experiencing pain, there's a natural tendency to want to withdraw. You want to run away to a dark corner by yourself or curl up under the covers and hide. You're done crying, finished trying to explain how you feel, and just can't stand being around people. No one gets it, anyway. You're tired of hearing how you should "snap out of it," or, "get a grip," and you're sick of being told, "It'll get better." You tell yourself, "If I could just be by myself and get away from it all, this pain will go away."

There's a big difference between the Painkiller of Isolation and the normal act of being alone. Jesus himself went away from others to be alone sometimes. He often wanted to be alone to pray and fast, and a certain amount of time alone is normal, healthy, and positive. The difference between the Painkiller of Isolation and ordinary "alone time" is that your "alone time" has a definite beginning and ending. It allows you to rest and recharge your mind and spirit, and gives you that essential one-on-one time with God.

THE START OF ISOLATION

In contrast, isolation becomes a prison. You feel that nobody cares. You're living in your own private hell. In order to escape your pain, you just get away from everything and everyone. You can even be isolated when you're surrounded by people. Many folks are there physically, but they've completely checked out mentally. Surrounded by their family, friends, coworkers, or church members, they have mentally and emotionally imprisoned themselves, refusing to share their burdens anymore because of the pain.

People are created for social interaction from the very beginning. Genesis 1 recounts the story of the Creation, explaining how God first created a habitat for humankind and the animals and then created all other living things. Everything He created He said was good, except that man was alone—there was no suitable companion found for him among the rest of creation. God put the man,

Adam, to sleep, and removed one of his ribs, using it to create woman.

Genesis 1:27–28 says as follows:

So God created man in His own image; in the image of God He created him; male and female He created them. Then God blessed them, and God said to them, "Be fruitful and multiply; fill the earth and subdue it; have dominion over the fish of the sea, over the birds of the air, and over every living thing that moves on the earth."

Here, God establishes the concept of community, family, and social interaction among people.

Community enhances our life and protects us. Conversely, isolation is a form of bondage and imprisonment. We have a culture of isolation today. From withdrawing into the Internet and social media to isolating ourselves using headphones to drown out those around us, we can easily withdraw into physical, emotional, or psychological isolation, even when surrounded by other people.

People, even imperfect and sometimes annoying people, serve a crucial purpose in our lives. God uses people to speak wisdom and perspective into our lives. As the saying goes, "Everyone on earth knows something you don't." That means you can literally learn something from every other person on earth!

This sense of community is especially important when we are in pain. When you are tired, broken, or emotionally weak, others are there to lift you up, encourage you, and give you a reason to carry on. But when you're in pain, that is also the hardest time to reach out to others, even though that's when you need others the most.

Our natural inclination is to say to ourselves, "I don't want to tell anyone what's going on or how I feel. They won't understand. They'll judge me." This becomes isolation, and that isolation keeps you lonely, doubting yourself, and dubious of others—right where Satan wants you to be and God doesn't want you to be.

Isolation starts with some painful event that damages your relationship with God, your spouse, your family, or anyone else in your life. Relationships are the natural cure for isolation, but when healthy relationships are absent or get messed up, you withdraw (either physically or emotionally or both) and isolate yourself.

Isolation begins slowly. The painful event is the trigger that allows the enemy to come in and separate you from your natural support network. Satan convinces you that your normal, natural community of fellow human beings is actually the source and cause of your pain. This process of separation leads you into the darkness of isolation. People don't usually realize it's happening, because it creeps up on you. Slowly, the hurt causes you to withdraw into a place of self-imprisonment.

God has a purpose for your life. That purpose depends on your healthy relationships with God, with your spouse, with your family, and with others. When any of these relationships are lacking or become distorted or perverted, isolation sets in.

You don't have to live in isolation! God created you for healthy, supportive, meaningful relationships with Himself and with others.

Unmerited Pain

Isolation begins with unmerited pain. You got hurt. You didn't deserve it, didn't ask for it, and it isn't your fault. Your spouse had an affair. You lost your job. Maybe your family got into a big fight. You were going along, doing what you were supposed to do, bothering nobody. Wham! Out of the blue, all you got for your efforts was pain. Unmerited, undeserved, unwarranted pain.

Unbalanced Inward Persuasion

Once you're in pain, you begin to talk to yourself, in your mind. Pain allows your hurt feelings to lead you into making unhealthy decisions. You persuade yourself you're the innocent victim. You start counseling yourself, blowing things out of proportion, and eventually lying to yourself about the situation, the person who hurt you, and the isolation you're using in reaction to the pain.

The persuasive techniques you use are unbalanced, because you aren't seeking a balanced input from others. You aren't hearing another side of the matter; you're focusing only on your own thoughts, feelings, and response to the situation. That leads straight to beliefs that are in direct contrast to what the Bible says.

Unbiblical Belief

The Bible tells you the following:

- "All things work together for good." (Rom. 8:28)
- "I will never leave or forsake you." (Heb. 13:5)

- "My God shall supply all your need according to His riches in glory by Christ Jesus." (Phil. 4:19)
- "No weapon formed against you shall prosper." (Isa. 54:17)
- "Yea, though I walk through the valley of the shadow of death, I will fear no evil." (Ps. 23:4)

But when you fall into the trap of isolation, you forget all God's promises and listen only to yourself. Well, yourself and Satan.

Research has uncovered many dangers of isolation.[2][3][4][5][6] Isolation leads to depression, higher rates of suicide, higher levels of stress, obesity, a long list of serious health problems, and even premature death. Studies done in children relate isolation to other issues, including failing grades and antisocial behavior.

2 http://journals.plos.org/plosmedicine/article?id=10.1371/journal.pmed.1000316.

3 http://www.sciencedirect.com/science/article/pii/S0277953612000275.

4 http://www.pnas.org/content/113/3/578.abstract.

5 https://static1.squarespace.com/static/531897cde4b0fa5080a9b19e/t/555601d9e4b0849a888ed857/1431699929973/toward-a-neurology-of-loneliness.pdf.

6 http://heart.bmj.com/content/102/13/1009.

God created us from the beginning to live, work, and play in communities. When He created the earth, He said it was all good, except for one thing: man needed a companion. From the day we are born, we survive only because other people take care of us.[7] Numerous research studies point to the essential nature of human interaction, documenting the devastating effects of isolation from the moment of birth.[8] Isolation is in direct contrast to God's perfect design for how humans ought to live.

THE SEPARATION OF ISOLATION

Isolation doesn't stop your pain. Instead, it becomes its own form of bondage, and in essence, whatever pain drove you into isolation is now holding you hostage. The isolated person ends up in a self-inflicted solitary confinement.

In Psalm 42:4–5, King David says this:

When I remember these things,
I pour out my soul within me.
For I used to go with the multitude;

---

7   https://www.psychologytoday.com/blog/moral-landscapes/201112/dangers-crying-it-out.

8 http://www.nytimes.com/1988/02/02/science/the-experience-of-touch-research-points-to-a-critical-role.html?pagewanted=all.

I went with them to the house of God,
With the voice of joy and praise,
With a multitude that kept a pilgrim feast.
Why are you cast down, O my soul?
And why are you disquieted within me?
Hope in God, for I shall yet praise Him
For the help of His countenance.

Here, we see David separated from his people, which leads directly to depression and anxiety in his very soul. Without the natural support system of God, family, and others, you are completely alone. That is when you become weak, like the defenseless lamb separated from the flock. Feelings of worthlessness set in. You become helpless and defeated.

This is completely contrary to God's purpose. God has a plan for your life. He has made provision for you to fulfill His purpose for you, and part of that provision is a strong network of support wherein you aren't isolated, separated, and defeated.

People aren't perfect. The people God uses for His work aren't perfect, and the people He chooses to send into your life aren't perfect either. In fact, all the apostles He used to found the early church were terribly flawed! Peter denied Christ three times in His darkest hour on the cross. Paul was on the way to kill more Christians when he met Christ on the road to Damascus. Jesus's own brother likely didn't believe He was the Christ until after His death and resurrection. Imperfect people often do hurt the ones they love. But God can still use them to bless you, and He still wants to use you to bless their lives too!

The enemy's plan is contrary to God's plan. The enemy knows that, away from your support system, you are easy to devour, like the lone sheep, away from his flock and shepherd, is easier for a pack of wolves to surround and take down. Little by little, the enemy steers you away from the very relationships meant to help you. One day you look up, and you're alone, surrounded, and in trouble.

Ecclesiastes 4:9–12 says as follows:

Two are better than one,
Because they have a good reward for their labor.
For if they fall, one will lift up his companion.
But woe to him who is alone when he falls,
For he has no one to help him up.

Again, if two lie down together, they will keep warm;
But how can one be warm alone?
Though one may be overpowered by another, two can withstand him.
And a threefold cord is not quickly broken.

THE SORROW OF ISOLATION

Isolated and separated from anyone and everyone who could offer you encouragement and support, the devil has you all to himself. His lies go un-checked, aided by your own negative self-talk. You tell yourself it just isn't worth the risk of reaching out to anyone who might hurt you again. You alien-ate yourself so that no one can judge you, your thoughts, your decisions, or your actions.

Now that you're all alone and you have a strong negative inner dialogue going full steam, the devil has set you up for even more pain. You've seen those documentaries that show predators on the hunt. Lions, tigers, wolves, hyenas—these preda-tors almost never attack a herd, because when creatures are close together, they're almost impos-sible to defeat. The predator instead isolates one from the herd. Then, alone and defenseless, the separated one is easy pickings.

THE STRATEGY OF ISOLATION

The strategy of your enemy, Satan, is to get you alone for three reasons:

1. <u>To neutralize your effectiveness</u> (You can't fulfill God's purpose for you when you aren't interacting with those around you.)
2. <u>To torment your mind</u> (With negative self-talk and demons telling you that you are worthless and all alone, your mind becomes a prison of torment. When Satan cannot get your soul because you are saved, he attacks your mind to make you ineffective as a believer.)
3. <u>To devour your life</u> (The isolation, negative self-talk, and feelings of unworthiness lead to a downward spiral, and no one can help you pull out because you aren't listening to anyone or sharing with anyone. As with the prey animal separated from the protection of the herd, it is easy for your predator, Satan, to destroy your life, your testimony, and your effectiveness.)

This is precisely what Satan does. His strategy is to cut you from the herd, to isolate and devour you. You are separated from anyone who can support you. Satan steers you carefully away from any relationships that could help you pull yourself out of this imprisonment. Now, you're in trouble.

When you isolate yourself, you are easy prey for Satan, who the Bible tells us comes only to steal, to kill, and to destroy (I Pet. 5:8). The psalmist David felt this deeply when he wrote Psalms 102:7–11:

> Lord, hear my prayer! Listen to my plea! Don't turn away from me in this time of my distress. Bend down your ear and give me speedy answers, for my days disappear like smoke. My health is broken, and my heart is sick; it is trampled like grass and is withered. My food is tasteless, and I have lost my appetite. I am reduced to skin and bones because of all my groaning and despair. I am like a vulture in a far-off wilderness or like an owl alone in the desert. I lie awake, lonely as a solitary sparrow on the roof.

The Stronghold of Isolation

Once you're isolated and under demonic attack, Satan convinces you this is normal. After all, if you think it's normal, there's no reason to fix it, right? You are now blinded to the lies of Satan, and you are a prisoner of your isolation, living in a self-imposed solitary confinement. You accept this is just how life is. But God doesn't want you in isolation! Satan wants to convince you that the lies you're telling yourself about yourself and the lies the demons are telling you are all true. But this is not normal, and it isn't how God intended your life to be. This is Satan's stronghold—binding you to a lie and keeping you a prisoner in solitary confinement.

The Solution for Isolation

God is a relational God who loves you. He deeply desires a personal relationship with you and wants you to have healthy, supportive, nurturing relationships in your life.

So what's the solution for isolation?

I don't have one single right answer, because your answer will be different from everyone else's answers. When you're hurting, the last thing you need is some preacher saying "Here's my three-part solution" or "Just read your Bible." There is no canned, one-size-fits-all answer to pain that leads to the prison of isolation.

But I can tell you where to get your answer. Your own, personalized, tailor-made answer comes from the Lord. When Elijah ran from Jezebel[9] and isolated himself in the cave, he looked for the answer in an earthquake. Then he looked in the fire. Finally, his answer came in a still, small voice.

What is that still, small voice saying to you? Push everything else away, just for a moment, and focus on what God is telling you. Only you and God know the pain of your sorrows. God may tell you to cry. He may tell you to praise Him, or to lay down on your face and worship Him. He might say, "Be quiet and hear Me." What is God telling you to do? Follow His lead so that He can heal your pain and help you escape your self-made prison of isolation.

---

9 1 Kings 19.

2

Inappropriate Relationships

A man with a law degree claims to have fallen in love with his laptop. Having filled his beloved laptop with an abundance of pornography, he claims to prefer having intimate relations with the machine more than with a human being.

Identifying as a former gay, former transgender, now "machinist" (a term he apparently concocted to denote someone sexually attracted to a computer or other machine), Sevier has filed lawsuits in multiple states (Alabama, Florida, Texas, Utah, and Colorado) with demanding that they either recognize his marriage to his laptop computer (allegedly issued by the state of New Mexico[10]) or issue a new valid marriage license to this unholy union.

---

10 http://www.al.com/news/birmingham/index.ssf/2017/09/
mountain_brook_native_sues_ove.html.

He also filed suit against a baker, attempting to force the baker to make a wedding cake for himself and his wired bride, which he claims has "female attributes." Unbelievably, a judge has deemed at least parts of Sevier's lawsuit to have merit, allowing the case to proceed through the court system.[11]

Outrageous? Welcome to the sordid world of inappropriate relationships, where justifying most any behavior becomes acceptable.

It's time we all take off our church masks and get real about inappropriate relationships. Many of us, even pastors and deacons and choir members and regular church attendees, would say, "Been there, done that." It's time to stop judging others because they fall into different sins than we do and realize that we have all fallen short of the glory of God (Rom. 3:23).

Everyone's pain is different. Not everyone experiences the pain of a traumatic childhood or broken relationship or loss of a loved one the same way. There are people who lose a job and simply shrug it off as good riddance and go find another one. But there are also those who become devastated,

---

11 https://abovethelaw.com/tag/chris-sevier/.

fall into depression, and have trouble going on with their lives. No two pains and no two people experiencing pain are the same. Since we don't all experience the same pain in the same way, no single canned answer exists to fix all our pain.

Preachers and church folks like to say, "Just come to church!" or "Read your Bible!" But getting rid of pain isn't always that easy. You might have tried these things and still be suffering.

Though our pains are as different and varied as we are, we all have one thing in common: if we're running *away* from something, we're running *to* something. One of the most frequent painkillers we run to is inappropriate relationships.

Inappropriate relationships have been the downfall of many. In pain, people easily fall victim to things that would never have tempted them without that pain. But what they run to in their pain winds up causing them so much more pain. Inappropriate relationships devastate lives. Not only do they cause the people engaging in the relationships pain but they also lead to devastation within marriages, families, churches, and everyone related to those in the inappropriate relationship.

God has established the boundaries for appropriate relationships, and relationships outside these boundaries are demonic. James 1:13–15 says this:

> Let no one say when he is tempted, "I
> am tempted by God"; for God cannot be
> tempted by evil, nor does He Himself tempt
> anyone. But each one is tempted when he is
> drawn away by his own desires and enticed.
> Then, when desire has conceived, it gives
> birth to sin; and sin, when it is full-grown,
> brings forth death.

The lure of an inappropriate relationship never comes from God.

TYPES OF INAPPROPRIATE RELATIONSHIPS

Inappropriate relationships come in numerous forms. For unmarried people, it might be messing around with someone outside of marriage, living with someone you aren't married to, or even behaving inappropriately with someone who is married. Married men and women often fall into the devastating trap of adultery.

Today's culture presents us with an entirely new set of inappropriate relationships to run to when we are trying to get away from our pain. Many young men and women run to homosexuality or transgenderism. This happens so often in a young person's life because of so many different kinds of pain, such as abandonment, abuse, bullying, or peer pressure. The Bible makes it very clear that God created two genders: "He created them male and female, and blessed them and called them Mankind in the day they were created" (Gen. 5:2). The world, following the lead of Satan, now claims there are as many as seventy-one different genders to identify with![12] How confusing for young people today.

Sometimes, inappropriate relationships aren't even sexual. In the workplace or in church, people sometimes get their feelings hurt at the boss or get mad when things don't go their way. They respond to that hurt with the painkiller of inappropriate relationships. They form cliques, engaging in gossip and backbiting and running everyone else down. These gossips have escaped into inappropriate relationships instead of facing their hurt feelings, and these relationships can be just as devastating to the organization as an affair is to a family. We even have a term for it: the "toxic environment."

---

12 http://www.telegraph.co.uk/technology/facebook/10930654/Facebooks-71-gender-options-come-to-UK-users.html.

A friendship that takes too much time and re-sources away from your family relationships is also an inappropriate relationship. Do you spend more time with your pals than with your spouse? Are you letting a friendship get in the way of your family obligations? When someone outside your immediate family takes away time and energy you need to take care of the spouse and children God gave you, that, too, is an inappropriate relationship. How about that cell phone? Are you spending more time checking e-mails, texting, and scrolling social media than attending to the emotional needs of your spouse and children?

Abusive relationships are also inappropriate. When God placed the husband in charge, He did not do so for them to lord over their wives and families. In fact, the responsibility of leading comes with an enormous burden—husbands are to love their wives as Christ loves the church, even unto death! (Eph. 5:22–33). Jesus would never abuse His bride, the Church, not physically or verbally or emotionally or any other way. Obviously, it goes the other way too. It's an absolutely inappropriate relationship if the woman is verbally, physically, or emotionally abusing her spouse. That isn't submissive, and it certainly is not glorifying to God.

THE RESULTS OF INAPPROPRIATE RELATIONSHIPS

No matter what form of inappropriate relationship you run to, the end result is more pain. Inappropriate relationships rip families apart and destroy churches. Affairs and premarital sex and homosexuality cause tears and pain, guilt and shame. How many people have ended up in my pastoral office for counseling, crying and telling me, "If I had it to do over again, I wouldn't." In many cases, all it took was dropping their guard a little, flirting a little, stretching the limits of a friendship just a bit, and—BAM! The next thing they know they've crossed the boundary into inappropriate relationships.

All of us just want someone to love us. God established biblical principles for meeting those needs throughout our lives. Before marriage, He set forth regulations for a healthy parent-child relationship (Eph. 6:1–4). When we're grown, He established the boundaries for a healthy, mutually satisfying marriage. God's Word also sets up an umbrella of protection for the entire family, in which the husband stands before God, under the authority and protection of a local church, providing protection and security for his entire family. As long as he stands under godly leadership at the church, the wife stands under his leadership at home, and the children remain under their parents' authority as they should, all their needs for love, attention, affection, and companionship are met, naturally and appropriately.

But a break in any of these God-ordained relationships can cause pain and lead to the painkiller of inappropriate relationships. We know that these relationships aren't God's plan for us, but we get hurt and let our guard down and get sucked in before we know it. How does that happen?

THE CHASE OF INAPPROPRIATE RELATIONSHIPS: HOW PAIN SUCKS US IN

Joe and his wife, Sue, were high-school sweethearts. They married right out of high school, dutifully supporting each other as Joe finished his college degree and his young bride pursued her goal of becoming a paralegal. Now, in their early thirties, Joe and Sue each have thriving careers, three small kids demanding constant attention, a home that forever needs cleaning and maintaining, and an active social life that keeps them busy most weekends. Joe is busy working, mowing the lawn, and coaching their son's little league team. Sue works full time, keeps an impeccable home, cooks all organic meals for the family, and serves on several church committees.

Though all their activities are worthy and positive, they rarely have time to connect as a couple.

Joe feels unappreciated for his hard work, and Sue feels overwhelmed caring for their home and children mostly alone. Soon, a nice-looking unmarried woman at work notices how caring Joe is about his kids. She begins admiring his skills at work, how nicely he always manages to dress, and begins commenting on how his wife doesn't seem to appreciate what a fine man she has. About the same time, their daughter's soccer coach starts complimenting Sue on how nicely she's kept her looks after having three kids. He listens with understanding ears as she bemoans how Joe never takes her out anymore and rarely even compliments her looks.

With stressful lives, busy schedules, and unmet needs at home, Joe and Sue are perfectly set up for entering inappropriate relationships.

It is important to state that there is absolutely nothing wrong with desire. Desire is normal, natural, and is God's design to drive us to find strong relationships. As we discussed in the previous chapter on isolation, God made us to want, need, and thrive in healthy relationships. What isn't from

God is meeting those needs and fulfilling those desires outside His established boundaries. Meeting desires through inappropriate relationships does not ease your pain; it only causes more pain.

Inappropriate Relationships Are Demonic

Inappropriate relationships are subtle. They usually begin when we have unfulfilled needs, and those needs drive us to temptation to fulfill those needs elsewhere, outside of God's boundaries for relationships. When you have unmet needs and feel that temptation, the desire is your alarm bell that something is wrong! Desire for a relationship is from God, but desire for something outside of His boundaries is not from God. Inappropriate relationships do not come from God. They are demonic. (See James 1:13–15 above.)

Inappropriate Relationships Are Born of Unfulfilled Needs

So often, inappropriate relationships start with unfulfilled needs. Your wife isn't talking to you like she used to. Your husband isn't complimenting you like he used to. You have needs that are going unmet, and you get lonely and hurt. Then, it's so easy to tell yourself that you need or deserve this inappropriate relationship. Similarly, people may say that they deserve this relationship because their parents didn't love them enough or their spouse abandoned them or they suffered some trauma that causes them pain. They want the inappropriate relationship to fulfill those needs and ease their pain.

Inappropriate Relationships Involve Misplaced Affection

With your fresh hurt from your pain and unmet needs, you begin misplacing your affection. The wrong someone gives you a little time or attention and you, in your hurt, open your heart. Usually, it begins quite innocently: some talking, some consoling and understanding, stroking a hand or touching a shoulder. These are your red flags that an inappropriate relationship is on the horizon. Then comes the thrill of the kill. For many, sexual relationships are all about a notch on your belt or something to brag about.

Inappropriate Relationships Involve the "Thrill of the Kill"

Inappropriate relationships involve the thrill of the chase. There's a feeling of exhilaration about "bagging another one." All relationships are exciting when they first begin, but the inappropriate relationship is marked by the thrill of tasting that forbidden fruit. When you are thrilled by the prospect of a relationship that is outside God's established boundaries, this thrill should serve as a warning sign that you've entered into something dangerous that will only lead to more pain.

THE RIGHT EXAMPLE FOR FLEEING AN INAPPROPRIATE RELATIONSHIP

Let's take a look at the right example when it comes to dealing with the initial temptation of an inappropriate relationship. It's always better to recognize and stop one before it gets started.

In Genesis 39, we learn the story of Joseph. He'd been sold into slavery by his own brothers and taken to Egypt. Pharaoh's captain of the guard, named Potiphar, bought him. Joseph served the Lord and worked hard for his master, and soon Potiphar trusted him with everything that was in his household.

But Potiphar's wife was attracted to Joseph and tried multiple times to get him to sleep with her. In Genesis 39:8–9, we see his response to the temptation of the inappropriate relationship:

> But he refused and said to his master's wife, "Look, my master does not know what is with me in the house, and he has committed all that he has to my hand. There is no one

greater in this house than I, nor has he kept back anything from me but you, because you are his wife. How then can I do this great wickedness, and sin against God?"

When she persisted, Joseph fled. He ran out, leaving his garment in her hands. That's exactly what we're supposed to do when faced with the temptation of an inappropriate relationship—run!

While there are many times that Christians are called to stand firm, be strong, and go to battle, when it comes to temptation, especially sexual immorality, the Bible is clear. Don't fight—run. First Corinthians 6:18 says, "Flee sexual immorality. Every sin that a man does is outside the body, but he who commits sexual immorality sins against his own body."

JOSEPH'S FORMULA FOR FLEEING INAPPROPRIATE RELATIONSHIPS

Joseph's success in turning down an inappropriate relationship is threefold, and we can follow the same formula when facing our own temptations.

1. First, Joseph respected his authority figure, Potiphar. In his response to Potiphar's wife, he said he could not do that to his master.

2. Second, Joseph blamed it on God. He said God wouldn't allow him to commit adultery, even though he was in great pain, sold by his brothers into slavery in a foreign land and separated from everyone he knew and loved. Not even this could cause him to displease his God.

3. Thirdly, Joseph took his eyes off the woman and put them on God. When you keep your eyes on God instead of staring and lusting after sin, you have the fortitude to withstand temptations. You have to be willing to say, no matter how good they look or smell or how smart or sweet they are, that your first loyalty is to God.

THE CHARM OF INAPPROPRIATE RELATIONSHIPS: SAMSON AND DELILAH

Joseph is our example of the right way to handle the temptation of inappropriate relationships, but our poster boy for doing it wrong is Samson (Judg. 15–16). Samson was a judge of Israel and a Nazarite. One of his Nazarite vows was that he would never cut his hair. For his obedience, God endowed Samson with superhuman strength. But Delilah sided with the Philistines over Samson and tried several times to use her womanly charms to find out what the source of his strength was in order to tell his enemies, the Philistines, so that they could defeat him.

Delilah kept after him, tormenting him day and night. She sweet talked him and stroked him and made him totally miserable! Three times he lied to her, until she finally wooed him into telling her the true source of his strength—his long hair, which had never been cut. She immediately told the Philistines, who came in and defeated Samson. He paid for caving in to her seduction with his life.

In the same way that Delilah charmed Samson into giving her his secret, Satan is trying to charm you into destroying your life. We are told in the ending of that story that the Lord departed from Samson. Once we cave in to Satan's temptations, we lose the strength of God and become vulnerable to sin, just as Samson did when he gave in to Delilah the seductress and allowed his hair to be cut.

THE CATCH OF INAPPROPRIATE RELATIONSHIPS: DAVID AND BATHSHEBA

Delilah represents the charm of inappropriate relationships, and Bathsheba represents the catch of inappropriate relationships. In 2 Samuel 11:1–5, we read about King David. Instead of leading his troops into battle like he was supposed to, he stayed home and took a nap. When he got up, he looked out the window and beheld Bathsheba, bathing on her rooftop, in plain sight of the king's bedchamber. He sent for her and they had sex, and she got pregnant.

The Bible says, "Be sure your sins will find you out" (Num. 32:23), and that was certainly true in David's case. In order to cover up his adultery, he ended up committing murder. When Bathsheba told David she was pregnant, he had her husband (who was one of his mightiest fighting soldiers) brought home, in the hopes he'd sleep with his wife and cover the pregnancy. But Uriah was a strong leader and refused to enjoy his wife at home while his men were dying on the battlefield. So David sent him to the front lines of the battle, where he was sure to be killed. Because of David's sins, the child became very sick and died. Your pain does not get better when you get in an inappropriate relationship. Instead, it gets much, much worse.

David suffered the consequences of his inappropriate relationship with Bathsheba. Though his short-term experience was pleasure, in the long term, it was only regret and more pain.

After Uriah's death, Bathsheba took her required mourning time and then joined David in his palace to be his wife. David thought it was all over. But God sent the prophet Nathan to confront David. David repented of his sins, but as a punishment, the child born to David and Bathsheba died when he was just seven days old.

David illustrates the consequences of inappropriate relationships.

1. In the short term, there is pleasure, but pleasure soon turns to guilt and conviction. David had fun for a moment with Bathsheba, but soon that fun turned into fear over getting caught.
2. In the mid term, inappropriate relationships lead to blame, justifying, and trying to hide, as David did when he tried to cover up his sins by calling Uriah off the battlefield and subsequently having him murdered.
3. In the long term, there is always exposure: people find out. This is a time of intense regret, as David went through when he was confronted by Nathan the prophet and when he had to watch his child fall sick and die. James 1:15 explains this process:

"Then, when desire has conceived, it gives birth to sin; and sin, when it is full-grown, brings forth death." Inappropriate relationships cause untold pain, not just pain for you, but pain for your family, the other person's family, your friends, and the church; everyone around an inappropriate relationship is affected by pain.

You can read about David's pain in his own words in Psalms 32:3–4 (NKJV):

When I kept silent, my bones grew old
Through my groaning all the day long.
For day and night Your hand was heavy upon me;
My vitality was turned into the drought of summer.

THE CURE FOR INAPPROPRIATE RELATIONSHIPS

So what is the cure? How can you fix it if you're close to becoming involved or are already involved in an inappropriate relationship?

There is only one way out of the devastating painkiller of inappropriate relationships, and it's a three-step process:

1. *Confession*—You have to own up to it and admit what's going on. Start by confessing to God. If you need to, also confess to your spouse, your pastor, your family, or whomever you have hurt with your inappropriate relationship.

2. *Repentance*—You have to turn away from the inappropriate relationship. God can't bless what isn't ordained of Him. You cannot build a house on an unstable foundation. God will not bless sin, but He is faithful and just to forgive us of our sins (1 John 1:9). Come to the throne and obtain mercy.

3. *An exchanged life*—You have to exchange your inappropriate relationship for His new life. God is the God of second chances, third chances, gazillion chances. Put away your inappropriate relationship for a walk with Him. He isn't just a painkiller, He is our Pain Taker!

You haven't gone too far! John 8:1–11 tells the story of Jesus after he preached on the Mount of Olives and came to the temple. While he was teaching and expounding on scripture, the religious men brought in a woman caught in adultery. They brought her in front of everyone. She was guilty. The law of Moses said to stone her. The religious men sought to trap Jesus into going against the law of Moses.

After hearing their accusations, He said, "Those of you without sin, cast the first stone." In other words, if you're so perfect, be the first to throw a rock. They were convicted, and they left. Jesus did not condemn her, nor did He allow the religious elite to condemn her.

Where you run when you're in pain may be different than where someone else runs, but one is no better than the other. Whether your painkiller is drug addiction, an independent spirit, isolation, or inappropriate relationships, when you confess and repent, there is redemption. Jesus said to the woman caught in adultery, "Where are your accusers? Has no man condemned you? Neither do I condemn you, go and sin no more."

Are you thinking, "I sure am glad I'm not one of those people?" What about the lust you have hidden in your heart? Are you wearing your church mask? We are the bride of Christ, not just girlfriends. Have you been unfaithful or disloyal to Christ? Have you allowed something else into your life, that you love more than you love Him? That's an inappropriate relationship.

Anything that takes the place of God in our life is an inappropriate relationship. When you're hurting and you run to the wrong thing, you must confess, repent, and get the joy back in your life! Go and sin no more. The same God who forgave the woman caught in adultery will heal you today. God will take your pain if you give it to Him, your ultimate Pain Taker.

3

Independent Spirit

Little Molly was four years old. Called to the family dinner table, she was neither hungry nor in the mood to comply with her parents' wishes that she seat herself. Her dad said, "Molly, sit down. We're ready to eat."

Molly replied, "No, Daddy. I don't want to!" After several such exchanges, her dad finally had enough.

"Molly! I said sit down, or I will discipline you!" Molly, still not wanting to sit, but fearing punishment, finally sat down. Her dad said, "Now see? Was that so bad?"

Molly replied, "I may be sitting down on the outside, but I'm still standing up on the inside!"

While humorous, we can all relate to Molly's spirit of independence. We may have to comply on the outside, but on the inside we're still doing what we want to do. That's the rebellious, self-willed Independent Spirit.

Whether you are old or young, rich or poor, big or little, you will have pain in this life. Christians sometimes mistakenly believe that pain and troubles in a person's life mean that they've sinned or somehow displeased God. They associate pain with punishment or a lack of blessing due to some sin or shortcoming.

In reality, nothing could be further from the truth. In Proverbs 3:12, King Solomon tells us, "For whom the Lord loves He corrects, Just as a father the son in whom he delights." This point is repeated by Paul in Hebrews 12:6, when he writes, "For whom the Lord loves He chastens, And scourges every son whom He receives." Jesus Himself told us in John 16:33, "These things I have spoken to you, that in Me you may have peace. In the world you will have tribulation; but be of good cheer, I have overcome the world."

Our usual response to pain is to run—to get away. When you accidentally get too close to the hot stove, your reflexes jerk your hand away before you consciously think about it. Your foot instinctively reels from a stubbed toe or stepping on a LEGO. Similarly, our minds and our hearts reflexively retreat from mental and emotional pain.

As I've said before, when you run *from* something, you're always running *to* something. When you run to Jesus with your pain, that pain produces the Fruits of the Spirit: love, joy, peace, long-suffering, kindness, goodness, faithfulness, gentleness, and self-control. But there are many other painkillers people run to instead of the loving, welcoming arms of Jesus. The wrong painkillers only lead to more pain.

WHAT IS THE INDEPENDENT SPIRIT?

We've talked about running to isolation and running to inappropriate relationships. But another common painkiller is the independent spirit. This painkiller is much more subtle. It's obvious when a person isolates himself or herself or engages in inappropriate relationships, but it's less obvious when they engage in an independent spirit.

An independent spirit is one that won't listen. They don't need your advice or input. This attitude is expressed articulately in the iconic Frank Sinatra song, "My Way." Each stanza of the song talks about what the singer has been through during his life and ends by repeating at the end of each stanza how he did it "my way."

> Yes, there were times, I'm sure you knew
> When I bit off more than I could chew
> But through it all, when there was doubt
> I ate it up and spit it out
> I faced it all and I stood tall
> And did it my way.

The independent spirit is rooted in pride. It is a spirit of rebellion, leading us away from the umbrella of protection established by God. What begins as pain and grows into the independent spirit of "I don't need anyone else anymore" soon becomes a spirit of poison. It culminates in a person who is rude, bitter, mean, rebellious, cold hearted, and smug and blames others for all his or her problems. The end result is that the independent spirit destroys your life, your relationships, your testimony, your family, and potentially your career and even your church.

THE BEGINNING OF THE INDEPENDENT SPIRIT

The Bible is filled with stories of people who fell into the trap of the independent spirit. The nation of Israel, for instance, is a good example of how this spirit is born and how it looks when full grown.

The Israelites moved to the land of Egypt while they were still a small group of just seventy people. As they grew in numbers, the Egyptians were afraid that Israel would eventually outnumber them and take them over. So they enslaved them.

Israel served the Egyptians as slaves for four hundred years, until God sent Moses to free them. During that time, God performed ten of the greatest miracles in history—a series of plagues that showed Pharaoh and Egypt His power and glory. After the Israelites were freed, God performed another series of incredible miracles, including the parting of the Red Sea, sending manna from heaven to feed them each day, and giving them a pillar of fire to guide them at night and a cloud to protect and guide them during the day. Still, they soon forgot what a loving, caring, and powerful God was behind them.

Soon, they began complaining. They complained about getting tired of eating manna. They grumbled about their leader, Moses. They worried about not having enough water out in the desert. Within days of Moses going up Mount Sinai to receive the Ten Commandments, they were worshiping a golden calf, made from their own jewelry by their priest, Aaron. In their fear and pain, they forgot the many wonderful miracles of God and turned to an independent spirit of grumbling, complaining, and doing things their own way instead of God's way. This independent spirit resulted in their punishment of wandering the desert for forty years, unable to inhabit their Promised Land.

The independent spirit starts when you get hurt and respond by closing yourself off to others. For example, the Israelites became fearful, even though they had seen the miracles of God. They allowed themselves to become dissatisfied with their food, worried over water, and anxious about the capabilities of their leadership.

There is a huge difference between the painkiller of the independent spirit and the admirable quality of determination. The determined spirit is driven to move forward and push toward achieving goals and success. The painkiller independent spirit instead steps out from under God's protective umbrella.

GOD'S ORDAINED UMBRELLA OF PROTECTION

Jesus holds the umbrella of the church. As long as Christians stand under the protection of the church, including the authority of their pastor and the fellowship and accountability of the congregation, they are protected from the fiery darts of the devil. But once they step outside the protection of that authority, fellowship, and accountability, and lean to their own independent spirit for answers, that protective umbrella no longer stops the devil's darts. When you step out from under this umbrella, you're not just exposing yourself to Satan's attacks. You're exposing your whole family! Now your independent spirit causes you more pain, and your entire family suffers right along with you.

THE REASON FOR THE INDEPENDENT SPIRIT

Like so many of our issues, it all started with the rebellion of Satan. When humankind, represented by Adam and Eve, decided to follow Satan instead of God in the Garden of Eden,[13] that sinful, rebellious nature infected us and continues to drive us today. That fleshly nature is most pronounced when we are in pain.

We can read about how the devil initiated the independent spirit in Isaiah 14:12–14:

How you are fallen from heaven,
O Lucifer, son of the morning!

---

13 Genesis 1.

How you are cut down to the ground,
You who weakened the nations!
For you have said in your heart:
"I will ascend into heaven,
I will exalt my throne above the stars of God;
I will also sit on the mount of the congregation
On the farthest sides of the north;
I will ascend above the heights of the clouds,
I will be like the Most High."

God established creation so that we would all be in fellowship, enriching each other with advice, teaching, differing viewpoints, varied backgrounds, and other perspectives. But Satan chose an independent spirit that sought to elevate himself above the Most High God. This self-promotion didn't promote Satan, and it won't promote you! It demoted Satan (verse 12: "You are cut down to the ground."), and it will demote you. An independent spirit also derails God's purpose in your life. When you step outside the flock meant for your companionship and protection, you are wide open to the wiles of the devil.

When Adam and Eve listened to their own hearts and Satan's lies, being willingly deceived by the serpent in the Garden of Eden, they introduced that same independent spirit into humankind that caused Satan's fall from glory. Ever since, every human born has inherited and followed that same destructive independent spirit. (Rom. 3:23: "For all have sinned and fall short of the glory of God.")

Unfortunately, it leads to much more of the pain that we're trying to escape. The independent spirit is now part of our human nature. We have to fight it continually. When we get hurt, our natural instinct is to run away, quit listening to others, avoid being around people, flee from the authority in our lives, and, like old Frank Sinatra, do it "my way." We tell ourselves, "I don't need them."

When we get hurt, the independent spirit gives us an attitude. "Nobody's going to tell me what to do," we say. We determine to make our own decisions, without anyone else's advice, wisdom, insight, or perspective. For many Christians, the independent spirit drives us out of the church and away from our families. When this happens, and your independent spirit isolates you from your authority and support system, the devil cheers, because he's got you right where he wants you.

THE REALITY OF THE INDEPENDENT SPIRIT

There are three kinds of people in the world. The first is the Natural Person. He's never been saved, so he has no idea he's operating in his own flesh according to the will of his "father," Satan.

The second kind of person is the Spiritual Person. This person is saved, and is operating in the Spirit, not the flesh. When he or she gets hurt, they start asking, "What's going on, Lord? What are you trying to teach me in this pain?" Pain always leads the Spiritual Person to a closer, sweeter walk with Jesus and a victorious walk among family, friends, their church, their work, and others in their life.

The third type of person is the Carnal Person. This person is saved, but their actions, decisions, and reactions to pain are dominated by the flesh, not dictated by the Spirit. Paul talks to the "Carnal Christians" in Corinth when he wrote about wanting to feed them with meat (the deep truths of God) but instead having to give them milk (baby food or light teaching, because they were unable to hear and understand the deeper teachings of God[14][15]).

When you fall into the painkiller of the independent spirit, you are behaving like a Carnal Person, not like a Spiritual Person. Fleshly thinking interrupts

14 I Corinthians 3:2.
15 Hebrews 5:12–6:3.

the Spirit's leadership in your life. It puts you out of sync with God, allowing the devil to bring you devastation and more pain. Not only does the independent spirit drive away the loving support system you need to keep from making poor decisions but it also leads to making ill-informed and unwise decisions that lead to more hurt, heartache, and pain. There is wisdom in many counselors (Prov. 11:14, 15:22).

Some of the decisions Carnal Persons make when operating in the fleshly independent spirit instead of as spiritually guided person include those in the list Paul gave to the Galatians 5:19–21:

> Now the works of the flesh are evident, which are: adultery, fornication, uncleanness, lewdness, idolatry, sorcery, hatred, contentions, jealousies, outbursts of wrath, selfish ambitions, dissensions, heresies, envy, murders, drunkenness, revelries…that those who practice such things will not inherit the kingdom of God.

Carnal people easily fall into these works when separated from their support system. These fleshly sins lead to untold pain and heartache for the believer with the independent spirit.

e who truly care. Like this son, the indepen-
pirit doesn't cause you to grow and progress
tter yourself. It leads you, hungry and alone,
ecline that goes all the way to that desolate
n.

en you push people away and withdraw into
ndependent spirit, nobody likes you. Nobody
cares how tough, how cool, or how right
ink you are. You end up lonely and want-
he independent spirit ruins your spiritual life,
g you into the fleshly traps of the danger-
dependent spirit. Not only do you have the
asant personality traits to drive folks away
ance, hardheadedness, rudeness) but you
oon fall into many other temptations Satan
s at you, since you lack a support system for
e and perspective. This leads you into other
stating places, like the list in Galatians (adul-
fornication, hatred, discord, idolatry, jealousy,
h ambition, fits of rage, and more).

URNING FROM THE PAINKILLER OF INDEPENDENT SPIRIT

ou see yourself in this? Are you ready to get
Fortunately, there is a route out of the pain
devastation caused by the independent spirit.
begins by swallowing your pride. Be willing

THE RUIN OF THE INDEPENDENT SPIRIT

How does the independent spirit cause us pain and ruin? In Luke 15:11–31, Jesus gives us the parable of the prodigal son:

Then He [Jesus] said: "A certain man had two sons. And the younger of them said to his father, 'Father, give me the portion of goods that falls to me.' So he divided to them his livelihood. And not many days after, the younger son gathered all together, journeyed to a far country, and there wasted his possessions with prodigal living. But when he had spent all, there arose a severe famine in that land, and he began to be in want. Then he went and joined himself to a citizen of that country, and he sent him into his fields to feed swine. And he would gladly have filled his stomach with the pods that the swine ate, and no one gave him anything.

But when he came to himself, he said, 'How many of my father's hired servants have bread enough and to spare, and I perish with hunger! I will arise and go to my father, and will say to him, 'Father, I have sinned against heaven and before you, and I am no longer worthy to be called your son. Make me like one of your hired servants.'

And he arose and came to his father. But when he was still a great way off, his father saw him and had compassion, and ran and fell on his neck and kissed him. And the son said to him, 'Father, I have sinned against heaven and in your sight, and am no longer worthy to be called your son.'

But the father said to his servants, 'Bring out the best robe and put it on him, and put a ring on his hand and sandals on his feet. And bring the fatted calf here and kill it, and let us eat and be merry; for this my son was dead and is alive again; he was lost and is found.' And they began to be merry.

Now his older son was in the field. And as he came and drew near to the house, he heard music and dancing. So he called one of the servants and asked what these things meant. And he said to him, 'Your brother has come, and because he has received him safe and sound, your father has killed the fatted calf.'

But he was angry and would not go in. Therefore his father came out and pleaded with him. So he answered and said to his father, 'Lo, these many years I have been serving you; I never transgressed your commandment at any time; and yet you

never gave me a young g
make merry with my friend:
this son of yours came, wh
your livelihood with harlot:
fatted calf for him.'

And he said to him, 'Sor
with me, and all that I have
right that we should make
glad, for your brother was d
again, and was lost and is fo

Though the end of this parable t
flict between the two brothers,
was probably evident all along. T
er said, "Give me my share. I d
I want it now. I want it my way.
away from the authority in his lif
to wait on God, didn't want to v
pain or dissatisfaction drove him
in the first place.

The Bible says it didn't take m
prodigal son to run out of mone
friends. Like he was in the pigpen,
spirit drives you to waste and hurt.
hang out with and party with are c
until the money is gone. Then, li
son, you end up all alone, having

peopl
dent s
and b
to a c
pigpe

W
your i
really
you t
ing. T
suckir
ous i
unple
(arrog
also
throw
advic
deva
tery,
selfis

RET
THE
Do y
out?
and
It al

to admit you made a mistake! Now, you need to begin the walk back to spiritual health.

The walk back to spiritual health looks like this:

1. Revelation—In Luke 15:17, Jesus said the prodigal son "came to himself." He looked at where he'd been and where he ended up and had that facepalm ah-ha moment. It's that place where we ask ourselves, "What have I done? What was I thinking when I wasn't thinking?" Before, you had joy, love, and purpose. Now, you don't. That expectation that God is going to do great things has been sucked out of you. Friend, God didn't change, you did!

2. Repentance—Next comes repentance. Repentance involves swallowing your pride and taking the blame for what went wrong. Your pain wasn't wrong, but your reaction to the pain was wrong. The only way to victory is through repentance: Luke 15:18–20, "I will set out and go back to my father and say to him: 'Father, I have sinned against heaven and against you. I am no longer worthy to be called your son; make me like one of your hired servants.' So he got up and went to his father."

It's important to note the difference between verse 11 and verse 19. In verse 11, the son said "give me." In verse 18, he said "make me." You have to get to the point that you aren't in it just for you anymore. You have to be ready and willing for God to make you what He wants you to be. When you say "make me," you put yourself back into the hands of God. When you say, "make me," then true reconciliation can happen.

3. Reconciliation—In verses 20 and 21, the prodigal son's father saw him coming from a long way away. He had been looking for his son to return all along! The father ran to his son and kissed him. The son responded that he wasn't worthy to be called son anymore. But the father rolled out a fine banquet, put the son in a grand robe and expensive ring, and had a party! When God sees your heart and knows you are seriously repentant, you don't have to run to Him. He will run to you. He's not waiting around to say, "You stinking little brat!" He's waiting anxiously to welcome you back into the family.

4. Restoration—The father of the prodigal son sent his servants for the best robe, ring, and fatted calf to kill and hold a feast. What a

great God we serve! With reconciliation, we can have restoration. Then comes revival.

5. Revival—In Luke 15:24, we see the prodigal son's joy come back. He finally has peace and a purpose again. When we come back from our prodigal lifestyle of the independent spirit, we can experience authentic revival. We are now back under the umbrella of authority and fellowship we're supposed to be so that we are protected from Satan's fiery darts. You realize "my way" stinks! You're ready to do it God's way.

When you're in pain, and Satan dangles that painkiller of the independent spirit, saying, "You don't deserve that," he may be right. You may have been treated unfairly. But running to that independent spirit only brings you more pain.

The bottom line is that the independent spirit is NOT a painkiller! The devil may tell you that tuning out others and depending only on yourself is the way out of pain. But it isn't. It only brings more pain and, eventually, ruin.

To escape the spiritual poverty of the independent spirit, you must first know Jesus Christ as your savior. Secondly, you must become a member of a local Bible-preaching, God-fearing church. These are your comrades, your support system, your accountability partners, and your umbrella of protection against the fiery darts of the devil. Swallow your pride so that you can be happy again in the joy of the Lord.

4

Idolatry

Kim and Kale had a precious beautiful daughter. They threw their entire being into loving her, caring for her, and providing for her. Then, out of the blue, their baby girl fell ill. After multiple hospitalizations and many excruciating medical treatments, there was nothing more that could be done. Kim and Kale had to say "goodbye" to their sweet baby.

After her death, the pain was unbearable. Unable to have more children, Kim and Kale were simply unable to move past their pain. Soon, going to church got replaced with doing other things—things that didn't remind them of their daughter. They grew tired of hearing how they needed to "move past it" and began tuning out their support system.

Before long, Kim replaced her affection for her daughter with other activities. She threw herself into shopping, quickly running up credit-card debt that *the couple would be hard pressed to ever pay off. Kale, in turn, threw himself into his work to escape the pain. His office became his sanctuary, and his paycheck his god. He might not have been able to save his daughter, but by golly, he could measure up as the best worker his company had ever seen. Now feeling she'd lost both her husband and her child, Kim no longer had any reason to care. The only thing that gave her even a moment's break from her pain was finding an amazing new outfit or the perfect throw pillow to match her new couch.*

The couple soon lost each other as well as themselves, as they sunk deeper and deeper into their respective idols. The marriage could no longer last.

When I first started telling everyone I was teaching a series on painkillers, everybody's thoughts automatically jumped to drugs and alcohol. Narcotics, opiates, methamphetamines, and even "lesser" painkillers, like pot and liquor, are most definitely a problem in today's society. But there is another painkiller we run to, and in some ways, it might be just as damaging in the long run as drug and alcohol addiction. It's the "painkiller" of idolatry.

When we think of idolatry, we usually think about old Bible stories or movies about ancient times, when people kneeled and worshiped before statues made of gold or stone or wood. You might also think of modern idol worship, such as those who bow down to statues of Buddha.

But idolatry isn't limited to bowing down to a little wooden statue. Idolatry is opening up your heart to the wrong things. And anything that isn't Jesus is the wrong thing! When we're hurting, we think, "If I just throw myself into this thing or that thing, the pain will go away." We may want a new job or a relationship or some hobby, or perhaps more money or a new car—whatever. Now, Jesus isn't the Lord of your heart anymore. That thing is.

America today is filled with idols. We have comfort food, television, sports, our careers, shopping, and even our kids. Anything that's keeping you from being everything you can be for God has become your idol. I am not immune just because I stand in the pulpit and preach every Sunday. I have to watch carefully that my ministry doesn't become my idol. If I let my church programs or building plans or even writing this book become more important to me than my relationship with God, then I am guilty of idol worship.

Matthew 6:24 explains the problem with idolatry: "No one can serve two masters; for either he will hate the one and love the other, or else he will be loyal to the one and despise the other. You cannot serve God and mammon." "Mammon" here can be translated as "money" or "material things." Anything we serve that isn't our Lord Jesus can fit this description. Even good things can become idols. Is your kids' softball team or the latest Netflix show or keeping a beautiful home or that new bass boat or having the best job among anyone on the block more important to you than serving Jesus? What do you pick over reading your Bible or going to church or serving in the church? There's your idol.

Matthew 6:19–21 tells us this:

Do not lay up for yourselves treasures on earth, where moth and rust destroy and where thieves break in and steal; but lay up for yourselves treasures in heaven, where neither moth nor rust destroys and where thieves do not break in and steal. For where your treasure is, there your heart will be also.

THE CAUSES OF PAIN THAT LEAD TO IDOLATRY

When we set our affections on things above, we are never disappointed. When we set our hearts on things below, we are always disappointed. Nothing on this earth is lasting. Whatever we serve down here will be done away with. Only those things we do in the name of Christ and in obedience to Him will last.

Spiritual Vacancies

So how does a contemporary person in this modern-day world get sucked into the painkiller of idolatry? Perhaps you remember in science class studying how nature hates a vacuum. Any area that isn't filled with something—air or matter or water or something—creates a vacuum. The vacuum exists solely to suck something in to fill that empty space. This is how your household vacuum cleaner works. The machine creates a void, and the air and dirty stuff rushes in to fill the void, thereby cleaning your floors.

Our spiritual natures also hate a vacuum. When our spirit selves aren't filled up with God like we're supposed to be, that vacuum will suck something dirty in there that isn't supposed to be there. We are created to worship. If we aren't worshiping our Lord and Savior, we are putting something else on that throne in our lives. Anything we put on that throne except Jesus will cause us more pain and more heartache.

When people get hurt and feel pain, they want to find something, *anything*, to run to. When they run to something other than God, that thing becomes their idol. When you hurt, it's easy to open your heart to a counterfeit god. This is exactly what Satan wants. John Calvin once wrote, "Man's nature, so to speak, is a perpetual factory of idols."

Misplaced Lordship

This is called misplaced lordship. When we have pain and are searching desperately to get rid of it, we often struggle against His lordship in our life. Then the world gets sucked into that vacancy. Now, you're worshiping that idol. We've still got our pain, plus another big, nasty mess. You inject problems into your life anytime you put something other than Jesus as lord of your life.

THE COMMAND AGAINST IDOLATRY

What's the problem with idolatry? What man or woman isn't jealous if their loved one puts other things ahead of them? Have you ever known couples who had problems because one of them put too much time and energy into their job or maybe a hobby like fishing or crafts? It doesn't have to be another person to make you jealous. Anything that your loved one places a higher importance on than you makes you jealous. Indeed, God is a jealous god, and when we put other things on the thrones of our hearts besides Him, He gets jealous too. Exodus 34:14 tells us, "For you shall worship no other god, for the Lord, whose name is Jealous, is a jealous God."

In 1 Corinthians 10:1–14 (KJV), Paul tells us from a Christian perspective what angered God so much when the children of Israel disobeyed him in the wilderness, after He freed them from their bondage in Egypt.

> But with many of them [Israelites] God was not well pleased: for they were overthrown in the wilderness. Now these things were our examples, to the intent we should not lust after evil things, as they also lusted. Neither be ye idolaters, as were some of them... Neither let us commit fornication, as some of them committed, and fell in one day three and twenty thousand. Neither let us tempt Christ, as some of them also tempted, and were destroyed of serpents. Neither murmur ye, as some of them also murmured, and were destroyed of the destroyer...There hath no temptation taken you but such as is common to man: but God is faithful, who will not suffer you to be tempted above that ye are able; but will with the temptation also make a way to escape, that ye may be able

to bear it. Wherefore, my dearly beloved, flee from idolatry.

Here, Paul gives a long list of the sins Israel committed:

- Idolatry
- Fornication
- Lust
- Tempting Christ
- Murmuring (grumbling)

We could all agree that fornication, lust, tempting Jesus, and grumbling against God and the leaders God appoints are sinful. But of all these sins, Paul only goes back and warns a second time against one of these: the sin of idolatry.

In fact, when God boiled down all the Law into ten basic principles (The Ten Commandments, found in Exod. 20:1–17), the very first one was against idolatry! Exodus 20:1–5 reads as follows:

And God spoke all these words, saying: "I am the Lord your God, who brought you out of the land of Egypt, out of the house of bondage. You shall have no other gods before Me. You shall not make for yourself a carved image—any likeness of anything that is in heaven above, or that is in the earth beneath, or that is in the water under the earth; you shall not bow down to them nor serve them. For I, the Lord your God, am a jealous God, visiting the iniquity of the fathers upon the children to the third and fourth generations of those who hate Me."

It's important to look carefully at that last part, "visiting the iniquity of the fathers upon the children to the third and fourth generations of those who hate Me." Our idolatry does not just affect us. When you put something besides the King of Kings and Lord of Lords on the throne of your heart, you are raining judgment down on your kids, your grandkids, great-grandkids, and your great-great-grandkids!

This is a serious problem today. People can be right where they're supposed to be with God, going to church and studying their Bibles and serving the Lord. But then something painful comes along. You lose a loved one, lose a job, get a divorce, or get in a bitter family fight. You get hurt, and instead of running to God to fix the pain, you run to the world. You bury yourself in worldly things: your idolatrous painkillers. Now, not only have you stepped outside God's protective umbrella and put yourself in clear range of Satan's fiery darts but you've also visited punishment on your kids, grandkids, and great-great-grandkids! The nation of Israel was destroyed for this very thing (Jer. 44).

THE CHAINS OF IDOLATRY

John 8:36 says, "Therefore if the Son makes you free, you shall be free indeed." But Satan's gig isn't about freedom; it's about chaining you and putting you in bondage. While Satan cannot lock your chains of bondage again after you've been saved by the blood of Jesus, he can put those chains around your neck and make you think you're still in bondage. To Satan, the next best thing to a non-Christian is an ineffective Christian who believes and acts like they're still locked up in chains.

When we deliberately embrace the ways of the world, we open ourselves up to Satan placing those chains back around our neck. While he can't lock the chains again to put us back in bondage once we're saved, he can convince us that we don't have the freedom Christ bought for us. He's cunning and deceitful. He's pretty good at telling us lies we believe, because he's practiced those lies on our parents and grandparents and great-great-great-grandparents—all the way back to Adam and Eve!

Psalms 106:28–31 and 35–41 talk about the consequences of God's children joining ourselves with idols and deliberately embracing the ways of the world:

> They joined themselves also to Baal of Peor,
> And ate sacrifices made to the dead.
> Thus they provoked Him to anger with their deeds,
> And the plague broke out among them…
> But they mingled with the Gentiles
> And learned their works;
> They served their idols,
> Which became a snare to them.
> They even sacrificed their sons
> And their daughters to demons,
> And shed innocent blood,
> The blood of their sons and daughters,
> Whom they sacrificed to the idols of Canaan;
> And the land was polluted with blood.
> Thus they were defiled by their own works,
> And played the harlot by their own deeds.
> Therefore the wrath of the Lord was kindled against His people,
> So that He abhorred His own inheritance.

And He gave them into the hand of the
Gentiles,
And those who hated them ruled over them.
Their enemies also oppressed them,
And they were brought into subjection
under their hand.
Many times He delivered them;
But they rebelled in their counsel,
And were brought low for their iniquity.

Have you mingled yourself with the world and
learned to embrace their ways instead of God's
ways? When you do this, you dilute and pollute
sound doctrine, leading to even more pain in your
life.

The verse 2 Timothy 4:3 talks about this: "For
the time will come when they will not endure sound
doctrine, but according to their own desires, because they have itching ears, they will heap up for
themselves teachers; and they will turn their ears
away from the truth, and be turned aside to fa-
bles." When you separate yourself from God's ordained teaching, you begin listening to the wrong
things. Satan blinds you and lies to you, and you
start believing what you want to believe instead of
what God says.

Today's world doesn't want to hear about sin. They don't want to talk about the hard stuff. We live in a society of "eat, drink, and be merry," and this is especially our reaction when we experience pain! But this way merely sets you up for the bondage the devil wants to put you in.

What you do in moderation your children will do liberally. If you drink a little, your kids will indulge in alcohol, especially when they go through pain. After all, that's what Mom and Dad do. They have a bad day, and they sip some wine or beer or smoke a little dope, and it's all better. If we engage in inappropriate relationships a little, they'll believe that sex outside marriage and straying outside the family unit is the way people do things. They will be unable to sustain a happy, healthy marriage and family, because you taught them the world's way.

Kids are not stupid. They know what you're watching. They know you're sneaking around with pot or alcohol. They know when you're flirting with someone who isn't their mom or dad. Is it worth the horror and grief of watching your children struggle through drug or alcohol addiction, just to escape your pain now? If you think you're hurting before you engage in idolatry, just wait until you see your child shaking and vomiting from withdrawals, or lying on his or her deathbed, succumbing to AIDS. That's too late to wish you'd found a healthier example for them when it comes to dealing with pain.

Our purpose in life is to please God the Father. That was Jesus's purpose (John 6:38—"For I have come down from heaven, not to do My own will, but the will of Him who sent Me."), and as His joint heirs, it is our purpose. (John 12:26—"If any man serve me, let him follow me; and where I am, there shall also my servant be: if any man serve me, him will my Father honor.") Even when we are in pain, our number-one goal and priority should be pleasing our Heavenly Father. No matter what you go through, you should always ask if your decisions and actions and reactions are pleasing to God the Father. Idolatry, or following after the things of the world instead of His things, never pleases the Father.

What's the reward for serving and pleasing the Father instead of yourself or the things of the world? First, it's the everlasting love of God. The world rusts, corrodes, and crumbles. The things of God are eternal. Second, the things of God are simply better! The world's painkillers always come with downsides (addiction, guilt, sorrow, corrupting your children, destroying your trustworthiness, destroying your relationships and career). God's pain-killing comes with no downsides! No strings, no catches, no hidden costs. Just the joy, peace, and eternal assurance of our Lord.

THE CORRUPTION OF IDOLATRY

The Message Bible isn't a version I ordinarily use in my studies or teaching. But the Message Bible's version of Romans 1:18–32 is an excellent explanation of how idolatry corrupts and causes destruction:

> But God's angry displeasure erupts as acts of human mistrust and wrongdoing and lying accumulate, as people try to put a shroud over truth. But the basic reality of God is plain enough. Open your eyes and there it is! By taking a long and thoughtful look at what God has created, people have always been able to see what their eyes as such can't see: eternal power, for instance, and the mystery of his divine being. So nobody has a good excuse. What happened was this: People knew God perfectly well, but when they didn't treat him like God, refusing to worship him, they trivialized themselves into silliness and confusion so that there was neither sense nor direction left in their lives.

They pretended to know it all, but were illiterate regarding life. They traded the glory of God who holds the whole world in his hands for cheap figurines you can buy at any roadside stand.

So God said, in effect, "If that's what you want, that's what you get." It wasn't long before they were living in a pigpen, smeared with filth, filthy inside and out. And all this because they traded the true God for a fake god, and worshiped the god they made instead of the God who made them— the God we bless, the God who blesses us. Oh, yes!

Worse followed. Refusing to know God, they soon didn't know how to be human either—women didn't know how to be women, men didn't know how to be men. Sexually confused, they abused and defiled one another, women with women, men with men—all lust, no love. And then they paid for it, oh, how they paid for it—emptied of God and love, godless and loveless wretches.

Since they didn't bother to acknowledge God, God quit bothering them and let them run loose. And then all hell broke loose: rampant evil, grabbing and grasping, vicious backstabbing. They made life hell on earth with their envy, wanton killing, bickering, and cheating. Look at them: mean-spirited, venomous, fork-tongued God-bashers. Bullies, swaggerers, insufferable windbags! They keep inventing new ways of wrecking lives. They ditch their parents when they get in the way. Stupid, slimy, cruel, cold-blooded. And it's not as if they don't know better. They know perfectly well they're spitting in God's face. And they don't care—worse, they hand out prizes to those who do the worst things best!

You don't have to be a seminary graduate to know there is a God! Nobody has a good excuse. People knew God, but when they didn't treat Him like God and refused to worship Him, it led to confusion and silliness. They have no real direction in their lives. People pretend to know it all but are completely ignorant regarding life. They traded the real and true God for cheap substitutes. God said, "If that's what you want, that's what you get."

Then, it isn't long before they're living in a pigpen, filthy inside and out, because they traded the one true God for a fake god and worshiped the god they made instead of the God who made them. Then, people literally forget how to be a human. It's all lust and no love. According to Romans, they pay for it. God quit bothering them and let them run loose, chasing their own lusts and desires. That's where we are today—with rampant evil everywhere. Wonder why there are mass shootings and rampant suicides, bullying and terrorism, and an utter lack of wisdom everywhere you go? This is it—we traded the truth of God for the lies of Satan, and here we are.

Let's take a look at Romans 1:28 in the New King James version: "And even as they did not like to retain God in their knowledge, God gave them over to a debased mind, to do those things which are not fitting." What if God decided to leave you alone? Genesis 6:3 (NIV) says, "My Spirit will not contend with humans forever, for they are mortal; their days will be a hundred and twenty years." God won't strive with you forever. There is a point at which He will leave you alone, and as Paul put it, hand you over to your own vile passions and debased mind.

What if God stopped bothering you? What if He never spoke to you again? What if your heart grew so cold in your pain and idolatry that God said, "You want the world? You got the world."

You KNOW your idols are wrong! You know you're putting other things in the place where God belongs—on the throne of your heart. God does not ask that you deny your pain. He only asks that you bring your pain to Him, confess your sins of idolatry, and surrender to Him and Him only.

In my sermons and Bible studies, I always give my listeners the bottom line. So what's the bottom line here? Idolatry is NOT a painkiller! You will never make your pain better by giving your heart over to the wrong thing. We are ALL guilty of letting the wrong thing get on the throne of our hearts from time to time. You only need to come to the Father, confess that you're guilty of chasing the wrong things, and ask for His forgiveness.

1 John 1:9 says, "If we confess our sins, He is faithful and just to forgive us our sins and to cleanse us from all unrighteousness." There are no strings. No hidden costs. No holding your past sins over your head. But you have to get honest with Him and tell Him you need Him more than anything else in your life.

Isaiah 53:4–5 speaks of the sacrifice and redemption of Christ some seven hundred years before Jesus was born as a man on this earth:

Surely He has borne our griefs
And carried our sorrows;
Yet we esteemed Him stricken,
Smitten by God, and afflicted.
But He was wounded for our transgressions,
He was bruised for our iniquities;
The chastisement for our peace was upon
Him,
And by His stripes we are healed.

By His stripes, we are healed. Abandon your idols and come to your ultimate painkiller and Pain Taker—Jesus Christ.

5

Intoxication

*E*mily's parents were never abusive. Probably because they weren't ever around. A latchkey kid from an early age, Emily knew to never watch TV or hang out with friends until her daily chores were done, including preparing dinner before her parents came home from work. Emily was lonely and sometimes frustrated, but she was basically a good kid.

Until one day, alone at home trying to finish her chores before starting homework, Emily heard a knock on the door. Thinking it was her friend stopping by early, she opened it—only to find an intruder on the other side. After hours of rape and torture, the intruder left, but Emily's pain never did.

Emily first turned to food to ease her pain, but that only led to fat shaming by her peers. To lose weight and cope with pain she couldn't deal with *and couldn't escape, Emily then turned to drugs. At first, it was "just pot." But soon, pot became pills and pills led to heroin, and heroin led to Emily doing things she never thought, as a middle-class girl from "the good side of town" she'd ever do.*

Now, Emily is ashamed to return to her family. The people she hangs out with aren't really her friends, and most are in worse shape than she is. After years of lying to herself, her friends, her family, and everyone else, she no longer has anywhere she feels like she can turn. She's all alone, afraid, and helpless. But she can't bear to think about all that. All she can manage to think about is where her next high is going to come from.

If you aren't in pain right now, chances are, you will be before long. We all battle with different things, but struggles and pain will always mark this lifetime. When I started this series on painkillers, I thought this sermon and chapter on intoxication would be the easiest of the entire series. Narcotics, drugs, pills, alcohol—I've counseled and helped people dealing with these issues for decades and that this one would practically write and preach itself. As it turned out, this one was the hardest of the entire series.

"Intoxication" is a powerful word. *Merriam-Webster*[16] defines it as follows:

- 1: an abnormal state that is essentially a poisoning
- 2a: the condition of having physical or mental control markedly diminished by the effects of alcohol or drugs

Different intoxicating substances cause different states of intoxication, such as an elated high, a hallucinogenic experience, or a numbed escape from reality. In other words, the intoxication produced by cocaine is different than that of heroin, alcohol, pot, or some other drug. But all produce an altered psychological, emotional, mental, and physical state.

What all intoxicating substances share is that root word hidden inside the word "in*toxic*ation." You're putting a *toxic*, or poisonous, substance in your body for the purpose of getting high, escaping reality, and numbing or running from pain.

Now, I'm not here to condemn or criticize those who are using perfectly legal prescription pain

---

16 https://www.merriam-webster.com/dictionary/intoxicated.

medications, prescribed by their doctor, that they truly need. Arthritis, cancer, bad backs, bad knees, headaches, and injuries: there are many painful conditions people live with, and thank God medical science has developed prescription and over-the-counter drugs to help us cope with these conditions! I am not here to bash legitimate, necessary use of prescribed medications in any way, shape, form, or fashion.

When we talk about the painkiller of intoxication for spiritual purposes, we are talking about problems with unprescribed abuse. This includes taking more than the doctor ordered, going to multiple doctors to get more than you're supposed to, buying or taking drugs that were prescribed for someone else, or taking nonprescription drugs or alcohol for the sole purpose of getting high. This includes both illicit drugs, like meth and heroin, abused prescription pills like oxycodone and Xanax, and legal drugs like alcohol or bath salts.

When you use intoxicating substances in an unregulated, abusive way, it becomes substance abuse. We are experiencing an epidemic of intoxication today. Almost everyone can tell you stories about lives that have been destroyed by substance abuse and intoxication.

THE SOURCES OF INTOXICATION

Intoxication is one of the most common ways people try to escape their pain. It's become the norm to unwind from a hard day with a glass (or bottle) of wine, or to drink beer to relax and enjoy the weekend. Even pot is now legal in some states and is socially acceptable even in places where it's still illegal. Got anxiety? Pop a pill. Stressful job? Take a drink. Need to unwind? Want to have fun? Here, have some pot or Ecstasy. (On a side note, the chemical name of the deceptively named Ecstasy is methylenedioxymethamphetamine. I don't even want to think about how many different toxic chemicals that represents.)

We could talk about the government declaring opioid abuse a national public health emergency.[17] We could list statistics, like the 88,000 deaths caused by alcoholism each year, or the 91 Americans who die every day from opioid abuse, or the 6.6 million children living with a parent who has a drinking problem.[18][19][20] But the point is very

---

17 http://www.foxnews.com/politics/2017/10/26/trump-to-declare-opioid-public-health-emergency.html.

18 https://www.projectknow.com/research/alcohol-and-drugs/.

19 https://www.cdc.gov/drugoverdose/epidemic/index.html.

20 https://www.usatoday.com/story/news/politics/2017/10/26/exclusive-trump-declare-public-health-emergency-opioid-crisis-partial-measure-figh/796797001/.

clear: we are paying far too high a cost for our intoxications. It drives up health-care costs, stresses out our emergency response teams, and fills up our morgues. But aside from the finances and resources these intoxications waste, intoxication is destroying human lives.

Nobody says before their first drink, "I'm going to become an alcoholic." Yet no one can become an alcoholic without taking that first drink. The same can be said of the countless lives destroyed by abusing prescription painkillers or illegal drugs like meth and X. If you can prevent the first time, you don't have to worry about the long, harrowing road back from a hard-core addiction.

Most people don't see anything wrong with drinking in today's society. After all, only about 30 percent of drinkers (approximately one in seven) actually go on to become alcoholics.[21] Maybe you can drink some and not have a problem with it.[22] But what if your kids can't? What if the little neighbor's boy who comes by the house every day and

---

[21] http://www.newsweek.com/30-percent-americans-have-had-alcohol-use-disorder-339085.

[22] https://www.niaaa.nih.gov/alcohol-health/overview-alcohol-consumption/alcohol-facts-and-statistics.

sees you drink tries it himself one day and becomes an alcoholic?

I love IBC Root Beer—greatest stuff in the world. One day, I was driving my truck, minding my own business, drinking my delicious IBC Root Beer in a bottle. Ironically, a bottled ICB Root Beer looks much like a bottle of real beer. Along the road, I got behind a school bus. In the back were a group of little kids, many of whom likely knew me as pastor of one of the churches in my area. How I felt! Knowing that those kids probably thought Brother Jacky was drinking a beer!

Now, what if one of those kids, thinking that the preacher did it so it was okay, grew up to become an alcoholic? What if he or she had an accident while driving and killed someone, all because I was careless? 1 Thessalonians 5:22 says, "Abstain from all appearance of evil." How much more irresponsible would I be if I actually were drinking alcohol? How would my church members feel if they saw me in a restaurant, sipping a beer on Friday night? Matthew 18:6 explains this quite well, "Whoever causes one of these little ones who believe in Me to sin, it would be better for him if a millstone were hung around his neck, and he were drowned in the depth of the sea."

Yikes! I don't want any part of that! That's why it is my rule, and the rule in my household, that we do not drink alcohol.

Some people mistakenly believe that the Bible doesn't address drugs, but actually the Word of God has plenty to say on the subject. In the book of Revelation, the very last book in the Bible, the apostle John is exiled on the island of Patmos, Greece. He's writing to describe the final events in human history, including God's inevitable judgment on humankind. Describing those who will be condemned to the Lake of Fire (hell for all eternity), John uses the Greek word *pharmakeía*. In our modern English Bible translations, this word is usually translated as "sorcery." But that same Greek word is where we get the English word "pharmacy" or "drugs." *Strong's Concordance* defines it as "the use of medicine, drugs or spells."[23]

Revelation 21:8 states this:

But the cowardly, unbelieving, abominable, murderers, sexually immoral, *sorcerers* [*pharmakeía* or drug use], idolaters, and all liars shall have their part in the lake which

23 http://biblehub.com/greek/5331.htm.

burns with fire and brimstone, which is the second death.

In other words, drug use IS sorcery! The "high" you get when you smoke or drink or take pills or shoot up is not just a physical reaction to the toxins you're putting into your body. It is witchcraft—open, unhindered fellowship with demons!

Paul uses the same word in Galatians 5:19–20:

Now the works of the flesh are evident, which are: adultery, fornication, uncleanness, lewdness, idolatry, *sorcery* [*pharmakeía* or drug use], hatred, contentions, jealousies, outbursts of wrath, selfish ambitions, dissensions, heresies.

Just like their counterparts, sorcery and witchcraft, drug use and other intoxications will produce painful things in your life.

THE STING OF INTOXICATION

While there are numerous sources of intoxication, the sting of intoxication is consistent. King Solomon, the wisest man who ever lived and author of two Old Testament books devoted to wisdom

(Proverbs and Ecclesiastes), had this to say about those who were bent on intoxication:

> Who hath woe? who hath sorrow? who hath contentions? who hath babbling? who hath wounds without cause? who hath redness of eyes? They that tarry long at the wine; they that go to seek mixed wine. Look not thou upon the wine when it is red, when it giveth his colour in the cup, when it moveth itself aright. At the last it biteth like a serpent, and stingeth like an adder. (Prov. 23:29–32)

Do you recognize these stings? Red eyes, babbling, wounds without a cause, sorrow, woe, contentions—all these are the common experiences of people who indulge in intoxication. You begin drinking or using drugs to cover up your pain, but you end up with bumps and bruises all over and no recollection of where they came from! We've all heard about the crying drunk ("who has sorrow") and the drunk who's ten feet tall and bulletproof ("who has contentions").

As I studied intoxication, I identified four stings of intoxication:

1. <u>The sting of conscience</u>: The very first time you become intoxicated, it bothers your conscience.
2. <u>The sting of self-worth</u>: Part of you knows you're better than this.
3. <u>The sting of disappointment</u>: You're disappointed with yourself that you stepped over that line.
4. <u>The sting of failure</u>: You feel you've failed because you turned to intoxication to try to numb your pain, and you know it will only cause more problems and more pain and never fix anything.

THE SEEING OF INTOXICATION

Intoxication also affects how we see things. The next verse, Proverbs 23:33 (KJV), says, "Thine eyes shall behold strange women, and thine heart shall utter perverse things." It's like the old joke about closing time at the bar: "the more you drink the better looking they get!" But it doesn't just affect your beer goggles.

Intoxication messes with your heart. The end of that verse says your heart will "utter perverse things." How many lives have been destroyed because drugs and alcohol messed with somebody's eyes and perverted their hearts? How many people ruined their marriages, destroyed their families, got in fights, engaged in crimes, and even killed somebody—all because they were intoxicated with drugs or alcohol?

When you wake up in the wrong bed or in jail, and you know you've done something terribly wrong, it's too late to say no to intoxication. How many people are living with broken marriages, unemployment, estranged families, and in prison cells, all because they got out-of-their mind intoxicated and made a stupid mistake they can't ever take back?

Whatever pain you're trying to escape from, intoxication cannot fix or heal that pain. It can only make things much, much worse.

THE SICKNESS OF INTOXICATION

Intoxication also produces sickness. Drugs and alcohol have a profound effect on you physically. Some substances can damage your health even in moderate quantities, especially when taken long term. A few of them can kill you or get you hooked the very first time you use them. Heroin is this way. Addicts can tell you horror stories of trips gone bad, the nightmare of overdoses, and the anguish of withdrawal symptoms.

Proverbs 23:34 (KJV) puts it this way, "Yea, thou shalt be as he that lieth down in the midst of the sea, or as he that lieth upon the top of a mast." Here, Solomon is talking about the sick feeling you get when you're drunk. It makes you feel like you're seasick, throwing up, nauseated, unable to stand, miserable, and unable to handle the most basic human functions, like walking or talking. The sickness comes from the "toxins" it takes to get you intoxicated. You are literally ingesting poison.

But the body oddly gets used to having those toxins and even becomes addicted to the substance. Now, the addict has to face a lifetime struggling with or battling against that addiction. Even *not* ingesting poison causes more pain.

THE STRONGHOLD OF INTOXICATION
Now we see the stronghold of intoxication. In the beginning, all you see is the lure of intoxication—it can ease your pain and make you feel good! But sin is only pleasurable for a season. Hebrews 11:25 says of Moses, "Choosing rather to suffer affliction with the people of God, than to enjoy the *pleasures*

of sin for a season; Esteeming the reproach of Christ greater riches than the treasures in Egypt: for he had respect unto the recompence of the reward" (italics mine). This concept is also stated in Job 20:5 (NIV) "that the mirth of the wicked is brief, the joy of the godless lasts but a moment."

Sin looks amazingly attractive from the outside. Otherwise, we'd never bite the lure. But once inside, it leads to Satanic, demonic strongholds. In addition to the physical, mental, and emotional problems caused by intoxication and addiction, it causes spiritual sickness. These strongholds become so established that even when you don't want to go back and use drugs or get drunk again, you do it anyway.

Once you're addicted to an intoxication, and that stronghold sets in, you cannot break it by yourself. You have to have help getting free of those chains that bind you.

Fortunately, you have a Savior who wants to liberate you from intoxication. John 8:36 says, "If the Son therefore shall make you free, ye shall be free indeed." Jesus is our Pain Taker and our Chain Breaker. There are 12-step programs and inpatient programs and outpatient programs and behavioral and cognitive therapies—all kinds of ways the world offers. But none of these are as powerful, as reliable, and as loving as the precious arms of Jesus Christ.

Some addicts tell marvelous testimonies of Jesus healing their addictions the moment they're saved, and they never want that drug or drink again. But many more tell of a lifetime of battling the addiction and winning one day at a time through Jesus Christ. But both will tell you of His love, His mercy, and His help in time of need.

Simply coming to Christ isn't the end of the lure of intoxication for most people. You also have to set your mind against it. Romans 12:2 says, "And do not be conformed to this world, but be transformed by the renewing of your mind,[24] that you may prove what is that good and acceptable and perfect will of God." This renewing process is not a one-time thing. It's continual, day by day, hour by hour, moment by moment.

---

24 Renewing the mind refers to our daily walk with Christ. Each day, we commit ourselves to learning more about Him, growing in Him, and walking with Him. As we do this (through prayer, Bible study, and fellowship with other believers), Christ renews our minds, keeping us ever growing in Him. That's what Paul meant in Romans when he talks about "transformed by the renewing of your mind."

You have to set your eyes and steel your mind on the things above, not the things below. Paul talks about putting on the Whole Armor of God so that you can withstand the devil (Eph. 6:10–18). When you wake up, His mercies are new every morning. But you have to set your mind on Him and His principles and discipline yourself to keep Satan from having a victory in your mind. You can't afford to drop your guard mentally, because once you're saved, Satan can't have your soul, so he goes after your mind. He wants to torment you mentally so that you can't be an effective, victorious Christian!

So, when the devil comes with his lies, you have to be ready with God's truths. Remind him "greater is He that is in me than he that is in the world." Tell him, "God is for me, who can be against me." Every day that you submit your mind and heart to Jesus, you gain a victory over intoxication.

But don't worry, because this battle will not last forever. When you go to be with Jesus, you'll get your ultimate victory. Things of this earth will grow strangely dim, and these earthly battles will be over. We will receive a body and mind like Jesus—perfect and incorruptible. Fight the good fight. Believe the Word of God. Honor Him with your life and your decisions, and He will honor you by fulfilling His promises.

And do not be afraid to seek help in this new walk in victory over your intoxication and addiction.

6

Intellectual Sabotage

Daniel was the smartest kid in his class. From an early age, he realized he could easily outsmart his teachers, his classmates, and even his parents with his deep mind and quick thinking. People started to resent it. Daniel was often excluded from birthday parties, left out of games at recess, and even bullied after school. He couldn't help being the smartest, and he just didn't understand their hostility. Whether they liked it or not, they had to admit he was always right!

Daniel eventually quit trying to fit in. Instead, he decided to use his superior intellect to get back at everyone who left him out, made fun of him, or did him wrong. He developed a sharp tongue, able to put someone in their place quickly and decisively. He was proud of his quick wit and used it to get his way everywhere he went. How dare some lowly department-store clerk or customer-service rep not give him what he wanted! He'd show them by making them look and feel like fools. They deserved it, and he deserved to get what he wanted.

This newly discovered talent alienated him even further from his peers. Instead of seeking a social life, he excelled in academics, eventually landing a great job. Yet he never was able to climb the corporate ladder, because his sharp words and superior know-it-all attitude made it impossible for him to get along with coworkers, clients, or his bosses.

Daniel eventually found himself all alone. Having spent a lifetime cutting others down to size to show them how much smarter, better, wittier, and quicker he was, he managed to drive off his wife, push away his children, and make himself completely unwelcome in his chosen field of work. Daniel retired, living on a meager social security income, deeply resenting how everyone in his life had treated him.

Intellectual pursuits and intellectual achievements are commendable. After all, the progress of civilization depends on these achievements! It is a worthy goal to improve yourself, develop your intellect, and strive for more knowledge and understanding. The Bible says "study to show thyself approved" (2 Tim. 2:15), and two entire books are dedicated to the pursuit of wisdom and understanding: Proverbs and Ecclesiastes. By all means, it's a godly and worthy pursuit to push yourself intellectually. When you stop learning, you stop growing.

But when we are in pain, it's a very easy outlet to escape into our intellect. We begin to evaluate our own value and worth by how smart we are. As the saying goes, "It takes more than intelligence to act intelligently." You can have all the smarts in the world and still be an absolute blooming idiot. I've seen it.

Pain can drive us to unhealthy intellectual pursuit that has nothing to do with bettering yourself or advancing humankind. When we're in pain, there's a tendency to want to get smarter than the guy who hurt you. You try to outsmart them and outsmart God and fix yourself all by yourself. You begin to believe you don't need other people, and you don't need God. It's the sneakiest of all the painkillers, but just like drugs, alcohol, and promiscuous sex, intellectual sabotage will destroy your life.

We can begin to understand what intellectual sabotage is by reading 2 Timothy 3:1–7:

This know also, that in the last days perilous times shall come. For men shall be lovers of their own selves, covetous, boasters, proud, blasphemers, disobedient to parents, unthankful, unholy, Without natural affection, trucebreakers, false accusers, incontinent [unable to control self], fierce, despisers of those that are good, Traitors, heady, high-minded, lovers of pleasures more than lovers of God; Having a form of godliness, but denying the power thereof: from such turn away. For of this sort are they which creep into houses, and lead captive silly women laden with sins, led away with divers lusts, *Ever learning, and never able to come to the knowledge of the truth.*

The italics in the last verse is mine, because that's what I want you to look at carefully. Paul was talking about people in the last days (which most Christians believe to be today) when people will become highly intellectual and build platforms on how smart they are but will be dumb as rocks when it comes to spiritual truths.

Society has dubbed this the information age. The body of information gathered by humankind is estimated at twelve hundred petabytes. Since most people can't possibly visualize how much information this is, picture it this way: one gigabyte is the equivalent of about seven minutes of an HD video. There are a million gigabytes in a single petabyte. What's more, our body of information doubles about every one to two years. We're soon reaching the point that simply storing and accessing these unimaginable quantities of data are challenging from both a programming standpoint and an energy standpoint. Worldwide, powering and cooling our data centers takes as much power as the entire nation of Sweden!

At the same time, we see lunacy in epic proportions. It's become so commonplace that we call ourselves (and each other) "sheeple": people who'll follow anybody anywhere anytime because they don't have enough sense to know better. We can't fix our energy problems, our violence problems, our medical problems, our financial problems, our addiction problems, our educational problems, or our diplomatic problems, yet we proclaim ourselves to be smart. The information age meets the age of idiocy.

The day Paul predicted only a few years after Christ's death has now come to pass. We're smarter than we've ever been intellectually, but we're dumber than we've ever been spiritually. We know how to reattach a severed limb, go to outer space, and split the atom—but we're missing God by a country mile.

But as the saying goes, "People do not care how much you know until they know how much you care." Your intellect does not impress people. Turning to your own intellect, without leaning and depending on God and His Spirit for guidance, makes you mean, critical, negative, destructive, self-righteous, arrogant, and a know-it-all. You may have all the answers, but you'll find yourself brilliantly alone. You might even become an intellectual terrorist—blowing up everybody with your perceived brilliance! You're the smartest fellow around, and everyone else is an idiot.

This, my friend, is a prime example of winning the battle but losing the war. "The way of a fool is right in his own eyes, But he who heeds counsel is wise" (Prov. 12:15).

Everyone, even Elon Musk, Stephen Hawking, and Bill Gates, is ignorant in some way. If I believe I know it all, I'm putting myself in a dangerous position. When I start thinking more highly of myself than I should, I begin to be critical of everyone else.

Intellectual sabotage happens to someone when they get hurt. Their self-worth becomes injured, and they start to believe they have something to prove. When the devil can set you up as a know-it-all, he can effectively eliminate any chance of God or anyone else being able to speak wisdom into your life!

Satan is a two-trick pony. He wins if he can get you to think more of yourself than you ought to or less of yourself than you ought to. When he does the first, he's trapped you in the painkiller of intellectual sabotage. When he does the latter, he's got you trapped in the painkiller of insecurity (see chapter VII). In intellectual sabotage, you try to prove or redeem yourself by proving others wrong, using your superior intellect.

INTELLECTUAL SABOTAGE IS THE OLDEST TRICK IN SATAN'S PLAYBOOK

What was the original sin? Yes, it was disobedience to God. But what did Satan use to tempt Eve and lure her into eating the forbidden fruit? Knowledge. The account is found in Genesis 3:4–6:

Then the serpent said to the woman, "You will not surely die. For God knows that in the day you eat of it *your eyes will be opened*, and you will *be like God, knowing good and evil.*" So when the woman saw that the tree was good for food, that it was pleasant to the eyes, and a tree *desirable to make one wise*, she took of its fruit and ate. She also gave to her husband with her, and he ate.
(italics mine)

Satan's first trick on humankind was to convince Eve she and her husband Adam could be as smart as God!

When we're in pain, we want to be smarter than God. We want to show others up with our smartness. We don't want to need God; we instead depend on our own intellect, and we want to use our minds as a weapon against God or anybody else who dares to hurt us!

INTELLECTUAL SABOTAGE IS FUELED BY SELF-RIGHTEOUSNESS

The Gospels recount many instances of Jesus interacting with people. He never called anyone names or put them down or raged at their sinful natures—except for the Pharisees, the religious elite of that day. He didn't yell at the adulteress or the fornicator or the ignorant. He only got angry with the religious intellectual elite.

In Luke 18:9–14, Jesus gives a parable about two men who went to pray:

> Also He [Jesus] spoke this parable to some who trusted in themselves that they were righteous, and despised others: "Two men went up to the temple to pray, one a Pharisee and the other a tax collector. The Pharisee stood and prayed thus with himself, 'God, I thank You that I am not like other men— extortioners, unjust, adulterers, or even as this tax collector. I fast twice a week; I give tithes of all that I possess.' And the tax collector, standing afar off, would not so much as raise his eyes to heaven, but beat his breast, saying, 'God, be merciful to me a sinner!'" I tell you, this man went down to his house justified rather than the other; for everyone who exalts himself will be humbled, and he who humbles himself will be exalted.

One was an intellectual, religious Pharisee, the other a sinful, hated tax collector. The Pharisee wanted everyone to know how much holier and smarter and better he was than the tax collector.

What did God think of their respective prayers? Jesus tells us in the next verse: "I tell you, this man went down to his house justified rather than the other; for everyone who exalts himself will be humbled, and he who humbles himself will be exalted." God doesn't think much of our intellect, and He certainly doesn't recognize or respect our self-righteousness.

The Pharisee shows us the danger of intellectual sabotage: trusting in yourself instead of God, as the tax collector did. You begin to despise others, thinking you're better than they are. In the religious realm, it shows up as "Look how spiritual I am, and you're not. I've got it all figured out, and you don't." Now, convinced of your rightness, Satan has you right where he wants you, and he begins to use that to destroy your life.

INTELLECTUAL SABOTAGE SETS THE TRAP OF SMART SUPERIORITY

The Pharisee in Jesus's parable didn't depend on love. He depended on his own goodness. When the intellect in your head becomes greater than the love in your heart, you're in trouble. Intellect must be balanced by your spiritual man, or you become like the people Paul talked about in 2 Timothy 3:7 (KJV): "Ever learning, and never able to come to the knowledge of the truth."

Do you see something of that Pharisee in yourself? "I'm glad I'm not like so-and-so. I'm glad I'm not like that drug addict or alcoholic or loose woman or adulterous man or that couple whose kids have gone crazy!" This is the Pharisee attitude. It's thinking you're better than others and looking down on them. What you can't see is that the devil is just setting you up for failure.

You can see the nastiness and unrighteousness of others' sins—like adultery, cheating, lying, extortion, or drunkenness—but you can't see the nastiness of your own sin of self-righteousness and self-promotion. In your pain, you've turned to a sin that doesn't look as nasty on the outside as some of the other sins. But on the inside, it is just as black, just as sick, and just as devastating as the rest.

It's important to note in Luke 18:11, "The Pharisee stood and prayed thus with himself " (italics mine). He was praying to himself, because when you have a superior, holier-than-thou, better-than-you attitude, nobody else will listen to you. Not even God. Psalms 66:18: "If I regard iniquity [sin] in my heart, the Lord will not hear me." And you certainly can't help anyone if you think you're better than they are. Even if you tried, they wouldn't listen and receive what you have to say.

Intellectual sabotage is so often born when some pain drives you to seek answers and protection from within yourself, instead of taking your pain straight to Jesus, who bore your pain and suffering on the cross.

INTELLECTUAL SABOTAGE IS SELF-PROMOTING

In Luke 18:11–12, the Pharisee promotes himself. He prayed to himself, about himself—"*I* do *this*, and *I* do *that*." When you're talking or thinking or praying, do you spend more time on God or more time on yourself? What does your inner dialogue reveal about what you think of others, God's children whom He loves and died for and redeemed?

INTELLECTUAL SABOTAGE GIVES BIRTH TO A STUBBORN ATTITUDE

Have you ever heard the expression, "You can't tell 'em anything, because they know everything!" That's the hallmark of the person who's hidden in intellectual sabotage to hide or kill their pain. It's an arrogant stubbornness that not only alienates you from people and relationships but also drives a wedge between yourself and God.

Over and over, the scriptures explain that when we exalt ourselves, God will bring us low, but when we humble ourselves, God will exalt us and lift us up! (Matt. 23:12, 1 Pet. 5:6, James 4:10, Luke 18:14).

INTELLECTUAL SABOTAGE IS SELF-GLORIFYING

What would the Pharisee's prayer sound like in to-day's language? "I'm all that, ain't I, God? Aren't you proud of me? I'm better than old so-and-so. He's a wreck, but look at me! I'm heaven's pretty boy. I'm glad my family isn't like that family. Just look how she's dressed today!" Can you hear yourself saying things like this?

This is what's wrong with our churches today! This is why people are leaving. Why they won't come back. Why they won't participate in our pro-grams. We think we're smarter, prettier, and better. This Pharisee attitude sneaks into your life, and you start to believe you're all that.

What you're missing is that we are ALL just sin-ners! There's nothing good about any one of us. If you think you're so smart, just wait until you run up against something you know nothing about. When something goes wrong with my roof, I realize I can't do it myself. I need a professional roofer. When something goes wrong with my car, I'm helpless! I need a knowledgeable mechanic. No one can be smart about everything. We need each other, and God made us to be interdependent on one another.

When you're in pain, if you get a brat attitude and decide to depend only on yourself and your own smarts, that's when you start messing it up.

INTELLECTUAL SABOTAGE IS SELF-DESTRUCTIVE

Not only does intellectual sabotage destroy your relationships with other people and God but it is also self-destructive. At the end of the parable of the pharisee and the tax collector, Jesus concludes, "I tell you, this man went down to his house justified rather than the other; for everyone who exalts himself will be humbled, and he who humbles himself will be exalted." All his lofty prayers did nothing for him. He left unjustified before God (and most likely despised by man). (Gal. 6:3 [KJV]—"For if a man think himself to be something, when he is nothing, he deceiveth himself.")

The tax collector, on the other hand, wouldn't even look up. He beat his chest and begged for mercy, knowing he was a sinner. He left justified before God. Intellect is a condition of the mind. Humility is a condition of the heart. God isn't impressed with how smart you are, but how humble you are. How do you think you could impress a God who invented, designed, and created such wonders as the complex dance of the solar system? Or the mind-boggling attributes of the human body? Or the powerful forces behind earthquakes and volcanoes and hurricanes, that lay waste to anything humankind can design or build?

When you hop on the I'm Smart train, you head to the station of Self-Destruction. You become critical with a false sense of superiority. You're setting yourself up for a fall. Proverbs 16:18 says, "Pride goes before destruction, And a haughty spirit before a fall."

Our bottom line is best illustrated in Matthew 23:1–12 (KJV):

Then spake Jesus to the multitude, and to his disciples, Saying The scribes and the Pharisees sit in Moses' seat: All therefore whatsoever they bid you observe, that observe and do; but do not ye after their works: for they say, and do not. For they bind heavy burdens and grievous to be borne, and lay them on men's shoulders; but they themselves will not move them with one of their fingers. But all their works they do for to be seen of men: they make broad their phylacteries, and enlarge the borders of their garments, And love the uppermost rooms at feasts, and the chief seats in the synagogues, And greetings in the markets, and to be called of men, Rabbi, Rabbi. But *be not ye called Rabbi*: for one is your Master, even Christ; and all ye are brethren. And *call no man your father upon the earth*: for one is your Father, which is in heaven. *Neither be ye called masters*: for one is your Master, even Christ. But he that is greatest among you shall be your servant. And *whosoever shall exalt himself shall be abased*; and he that shall humble himself shall be exalted. (italics mine)

In this scathing passage (you can read more of what Jesus said to the scribes and Pharisees in verses 13–33), He isn't talking to harlots or thieves or drug addicts. He's not talking to adulterers or cheaters or liars or drunks. He's speaking to the religious elite. The educated people. The "smart folks" of that day. He's speaking to those who have entered into intellectual sabotage. People who think they're better than everybody else. Better than others, smarter than God.

Is there a Pharisee hiding in your heart? Are you proud? Critical? Negative? Holier-than-thou? Convinced of your own righteousness and condemning of others? You may not do drugs or drink or run around, but the devil can still sneak in and set you up for failure, especially when you're hurting and looking for a painkiller. When you're hurting, it's easy for the devil to convince you you're smarter than God, smarter than those other people, and smarter than all your problems.

You may have all the answers. But nobody's going to listen. In trying to figure it out instead of trusting God, you merely push people away from you.

Have you been guilty of intellectual sabotage? It's one of Satan's oldest and sneakiest tricks. Do you need to repent of your inner Pharisee today?

7

Insecurity

Yvonne grew up in a critical, unsupportive household. Her parents were quick to say what she did was wrong, pointing out every flaw in detail, but they were slow with compliments and encouragement. Yvonne began to believe that she wasn't worthy of being built up.

In her hurt and pain, Yvonne retreated into a shield of insecurity. She felt like if she could criticize herself first, it wouldn't hurt so bad when someone else said something negative to or about her.

Yvonne didn't believe she was really worthy of love or appreciation or praise. She continually looked for anything and everything wrong with herself, filling her mind with negative self-talk. She quickly latched on to anything less than positive someone else had to say, all but ignoring any compliments or praise she was given. Often, *she even managed to turn harmless comments people made into something bad about her. It made healthy, functional relationships very difficult for Yvonne.*

Since she didn't believe in herself, her worth, her talents, or her achievements, Yvonne easily fell into a series of bad relationships. Though she desperately wanted someone to love and appreciate her, she easily accepted criticism, harsh and unkind words, and even abuse. Too insecure to believe in herself, she became dependent on her abusive partners. Worse, the pain that caused her to run to insecurity led to an endless reservoir for more pain and heartache in Yvonne's life. But she was too scared to believe in herself. She was hopelessly insecure.

Do you constantly fear more hurt, pain, and rejection? Do your fears and insecurities damage your relationships and cause you to feel worthless, depressed, and defeated? Do you have an inner dialogue that continually tells you that you're a loser, you never do anything right, and you'll never be good enough for anybody?

Insecurity is a common reaction to pain. Instead of a painkiller, insecurity acts as another source of pain in your life. Not only does insecurity cause you pain and heartache and damages your interpersonal relationships but it also makes it impossible for God to fulfill His purpose in your life. Whatever He asks you to do, you'll be hindered by feelings of inadequacy and fear of failure.

Insecurity also gives birth to unhealthy relationships. Feelings of inadequacy cause you to become involved with people you shouldn't. Or if you have loving, caring people in your life, insecurity nags at you until you become convinced you're not good enough for them and you'll never be able to please them. Either way, insecurity makes it nearly impossible to have a healthy, functional relationship with anyone.

Some insecurities are real; others are imagined. But both play over and over in your head, making it impossible to hear any voice that builds you up or gives you compliments. The insecure person feels like a failure no matter how much success they achieve in life. They feel inferior no matter how smart or good looking or talented they are.

Insecurity leads to fearfulness. You're always hiding because you're afraid to get hurt again. Once the fear sets in, it pushes you even deeper into your insecurities, leading to depression, defeat, and discouragement. Not only does insecurity make you miserable but it also makes everyone around you miserable too.

Insecurity also produces dependence. When you feel inadequate yourself, the natural tendency is to become dependent on something you do have confidence in. Now, your pain has driven you to depend on people or things around you instead of God. Then the devil gets involved, perverting your insecurities until you're miserable and fearful, unable to fulfill God's purpose for your life.

The sources of insecurity are as numerous as there are people who are insecure. Many insecure people come from a traumatic childhood, where there is no peace, but confusion, fighting, and arguing abound. Some people grow up in homes where there is never any encouragement. They're always beaten down and talked to negatively. Insecurity can come from failure or rejection. It can also be born of a trauma. Bullying is a common one, especially today, and can convince you that nobody loves you and nobody wants you. Too often, this leads to deeper issues, like self-hurting and even suicide.

All these pains are from the devil! Satan comes to steal, to kill, and to destroy, but Jesus came that we might have life and have it more abundantly (John 10:10).

Philippians 1:6 says, "Being confident of this very thing, that He who has begun a good work in you will complete it until the day of Jesus Christ." In this passage, Paul is writing to the church in Philippi, encouraging them, praying for them, thanking God for them, and hoping that they might live in abundance and joy, being overcomers. The first word here, "being," is interesting, because it denotes a consistent state of being. It means "to always be at" that place of confidence. Paul is telling Christians to "be in a constant state of confidence." Obviously, there is no place in that for insecurity.

Confidence is not boastful or prideful or arrogant. It's a place of consistency where you have total and glorious confidence about "this very thing: He who has begun a good work in you will perform it until the day of Jesus." That means that no matter what might come against you—even hell itself—but God is still at work in you.

You may not be able to see or understand what's going on, but you can always be confident that He's doing something, and that whatever He is doing is good. It's hard to see this in the midst of our pain and heartache, but it is no less true then than it is when we are in a wonderful season of life.

This is what you must remind yourself of and say to the devil when he starts whispering that you aren't good enough, you'll never get over this pain, that nobody cares, or you'll never amount to anything. Instead of letting these lies drive you into the pits of insecurity, you must learn to say, "Stop! I know that 'He who has begun a good work in you will complete it until the day of Jesus Christ,' and I am confident!"

You don't have to figure it all out. God's work and His confidence are there, regardless of your past, regardless of your bad decisions, regardless of your past failures. Not only is He at work—but He absolutely loves you! He loves you too much to give up on you. Your hope is built on nothing less than the blood of Jesus and His righteousness (not yours).

THE PROBLEM OF INSECURITY

In studying for this message, I came across three different characters in the Bible who had insecurities of their own that we can learn from. There are many more in there, but I picked three I think we can all relate to.

1. Moses

The first of our insecure Bible heroes is Moses. In Exodus 4:10–14, we find Moses meeting God in the burning bush. This incredible man of God, the man who would bravely face the powerful Pharaoh, the one who would lead the children of Israel in the desert for some forty years, the man who would stand on Mount Sinai with God Himself to receive the Ten Commandments—is telling God he can't accept his assignment.

> Then Moses said to the Lord, "O my Lord, I am not eloquent, neither before nor since You have spoken to Your servant; but I am slow of speech and slow of tongue." So the Lord said to him, "Who has made man's mouth? Or who makes the mute, the deaf, the seeing, or the blind? Have not I, the Lord? Now therefore, go, and I will be with your mouth and teach you what you shall say." But he said, "O my Lord, please send by the hand of whomever else You may send." So the anger of the Lord was kindled against Moses, and He said: "Is not Aaron the Levite your brother? I know that he can speak well. And look, he is also coming out to meet you. When he sees you, he will be glad in his heart." (Exod. 4:10–14)

Moses had a problem, and his problem was insecurity. Specifically, he was insecure about how he talked: he wasn't eloquent and had a stutter. Because of his insecurity and lack of faith, God strapped Moses with his brother, Aaron, to be his mouthpiece. Interestingly enough, it was Aaron who built the golden calf for the people while Moses was on the mountain with God, receiving the Ten Commandments.

Over the years, Aaron got the people into all kinds of trouble. Moses's insecurity led to God appointing Aaron, and that situation led to much pain among the people of Israel. Had Moses just put aside his insecurities and been obedient to God, perhaps Israel would have had fewer problems and less pain? When God approaches us, we have to be willing to say, "Here I am, Lord." He will work His divine will, despite our insecurities and protests. He's not interested in our excuses.

2. Abraham's Wife Sarah

Abraham, the great man of God who became the father of all the people of Israel, from ancient times to today, wasn't always so prolific. In fact, until Abraham was hundred years old and Sarah was ninety, they had no children. Sarah was barren.

Today, we have many medical treatments and other options for women who cannot bear children, but in that day, a woman's worth was largely relative to her ability to produce children for her husband. Over and over again, we see stories of women who were shamed and deemed less than worthy for their barrenness (Jacob's beloved wife Rachel, Samson's mother, Elizabeth the mother of John the Baptist, and Hannah the mother of Samuel, just to name a few).

Knowing God's promise that Abraham would become the father of many, Sarah, in her insecurity over her shameful barrenness, gave Abraham her handmaiden, Hagar the Egyptian, that she might bear him children and fulfill the promises of God. From this ungodly union of Abraham and Hagar came Ishmael. Hagar hated Sarah for what she had done in her faithlessness. Ishmael is the likely father of many modern-day enemies of Israel. It is impossible to measure the amount of pain caused throughout the centuries by Sarah's insecurity over her barrenness.

3. The Thief on the Cross
Insecurity over stuttering and barrenness are bad, but the thief on the cross next to Jesus was insecure for his very life! In fact, he had no reason for

security. Condemned to die, cast out by society, rejected by all, and headed straight for hell—the thief on the cross had nothing but insecurity. While many scriptures are dedicated to Moses and Sarah, we have but a couple of verses in which we meet the thief on the cross. At the time, he was hanging on a cross next to Jesus, and another criminal was also dying with them.

> Then one of the criminals who were hanged blasphemed Him, saying, "If You are the Christ, save Yourself and us." But the other, answering, rebuked him, saying, "Do you not even fear God, seeing you are under the same condemnation?" (Luke 23:39–40)

One of the criminals railed against Jesus, while the other expressed fear in God and insecurity in his condemnation. The thief on the cross was insecure about everything!

Now we see the problem of insecurity, but none of these problems started here. Moses's insecurity didn't begin at the burning bush. Sarah's insecurity didn't start the day she put her handmaiden Hagar in the tent with her husband, Abraham. The thief on the cross's insecurity didn't begin when they hung him up to die. Let's roll it back.

THEIR INSECURITIES STARTED WITH PAIN

Just like most of us, these biblical characters' insecurities were rooted in pain. This pain started years before. Things that happen "back there" cause us problems "up here."

1. Moses

Let's rewind to see how Moses ended up on the backside of the desert in the first place, tending flocks for his father-in-law. He was running from his past. In Exodus 2:11–15, we meet a Moses who has been raised as the son of Pharaoh's daughter, but who is actually a descendant of an Israelite woman, who hid her son to escape Pharaoh's orders that all male children be destroyed. Now grown in Exodus 2:11–15, he came outside one day and saw an Egyptian beating a Hebrew, one of his kinsmen. He killed the Egyptian and fled to a land called Midian, across the Red Sea from Egypt, to escape his punishment.

He stayed there for forty years, marrying, having children, and tending flocks for his father-in-law. That's when God came to him in the burning bush. But the insecurities that caused Moses to try to refuse God's calling really started all those years earlier, when Moses killed the Egyptian and fled from Pharaoh. The devil put a chain on him and told him he was a murderer, worthless to God. Moses's chains started way back in his past, when he murdered the Egyptian and ran from Pharaoh and from God.

Are you running from your past? Are you hiding your stuff from way back there? Are you tired of trying all your life to escape the pain of what happened in the past? God can't take you where He wants to until you let go of that insecurity from your past. He's ready to heal your scars that are hindering you now. You must gain a sense of security and worthiness so that you are ready when God calls you to do something.

2. Abraham's Wife Sarah

Like Moses, Sarah's problem didn't happen when she stepped out in faithlessness and gave Hagar to her husband. Her problem started five chapters before, in Genesis 11:30: "But Sarai was barren; she had no child." (Sarai was Sarah's name before God changed it in Genesis 17:15, at the time He also changed Abram's name to Abraham.)

In that day, a woman who could not bear children was a marked woman, worthless to society. Her thinking was that since her womb could produce nothing, she was nothing. In her insecurities, Sarah sought her self-worth the world's way, in a faithless act of trying to have children in a way other than God's way.

Have you felt like Sarah? Worthless? A Failure? Believing that everyone else has it going on, but you can't do anything worthy? When you feel that nothing good is coming out of your life, it's easy to fall into the trap of insecurity. But we still have God's promise from Philippians 1:6, "being confident of this very thing, that He who has begun a good work in you will complete it until the day of Jesus Christ." Even when we cannot have confidence and security in ourselves, we can have confidence and security in Christ Jesus.

Like Sarah at the impossible age of ninety, God can cause you to supernaturally produce.

3. Thief on the Cross

While Moses ran from past sins to his insecurities, and Sarah ran from her pain and shame of barrenness to her insecurities, the thief on the cross ran from the law. Do you have a criminal record? Have you run from the law and now feel condemned? Maybe the law already caught up with you and sentenced you.

I'm here to tell you that no matter what you've done, where sin abounds, grace does much more abound (Rom. 5:20). Jesus took your condemnation on the cross. While the Lord did not do away with the thief's punishment here on earth, He did take care of the thief's spiritual deficits. He promised the man in Luke 23:43: "And Jesus said to him, 'Assuredly, I say to you, today you will be with Me in Paradise.'"

The thief had no reason to be secure in himself. He couldn't climb down from the cross and be baptized. He couldn't go out into the world and be a witness for Christ. He couldn't study scripture or attend church or even tithe. His security lay solely on Jesus.

Many convicts get saved and have incredible and inspiring tales of how God worked miracles and set them free. But many more tell testimonies instead of how God worked with them through their incarceration and punishment. Like the thief on the cross, Jesus doesn't always make our earthly punishment go away. What He promises is that He will be there with you through it, as he did on the cross next to the thief, and that when it's all over, your sins are forgiven and He will remember them no more. (Hebrews 8:12—"For I will be merciful to their unrighteousness, and their sins and their iniquities will I remember no more.")

The devil wants to keep you insecure but not just here on earth. He wants to make you insecure about your eternity. Have you ever been hopelessly insecure, like the thief on the cross? Have you had only hell all your life, with no sign of things ever getting any better? Know this, my friend, that God did not create you for just this time here on earth. He created you for all eternity. He can help you learn to see the bigger picture: not just what's going on here and now, but what's going to go on in the hereafter.

THE PATH OF INSECURITY

In the beginning of this chapter, we talked about a few of the ways that insecurity is born into your life. Those ways are as numerous as there are people struggling with insecurities. But all insecurity follows something of a predictable path.

1. You experience pain.
2. Your pain causes you to become insecure.
3. The devil turns your insecurities into fear.
4. The demonic fear makes it impossible to have faith.

5. When our faith is interrupted, it manifests in unbelief in ourselves and in our God. We are now easily defeated, helpless, and hopeless.

Fear is not of God! The Bible says, "fear not," some 365 times. One time for every day of the year. He has power and strength and security for every day of our lives! Fear is the opposite of faith, and without faith it is impossible to please God (Heb. 11:6).

When you have pain and run to the wrong painkiller, the pain only gets worse. When you run to insecurity, you end up with the hurt of darkness, depression, discouragement, low self-esteem, and defeat. Like Moses, Sarah, and the thief on the cross, you become convinced you aren't good enough or you can't do this or that. But while pain leads to insecurity and insecurity leads down a deep, dark corridor, God has a blessed provision for your security!

THE PROVISION FOR INSECURITY

When we run away from God to painkillers like insecurity, we become mired in all kinds of problems. For Moses, his faithlessness caused immeasurable troubles among the Israelites. Sarah's insecurities led to the birth of a people still causing trouble for the descendants of her son Isaac today. The thief's insecurities led him straight to the cross, where, though he found redemption for his soul, he nonetheless lost his life.

God makes provisions for our insecurities and weaknesses. He doesn't expect us to stand alone to face our fears and insecurities. He is always right by our side, even through the pain and trials of life. This provision is illustrated beautifully in 2 Corinthians 12:9:

> And He said to me, "My grace is sufficient for you, for My strength is made perfect in weakness." Therefore most gladly I will rather boast in my infirmities, that the power of Christ may rest upon me.

In this verse, Paul explains to us the Lord's three-fold provision for our security:

1. <u>God's Grace</u>—God has shown us His abundant grace, undeserved favor, and unconditional blessing. Even when it feels like you have nothing left, you never lose God's grace.
2. <u>God's Strength</u>—Even Paul sometimes didn't have the strength to stand on his own two feet; how much more is that true of you

and I? But even when you can't stand on your own, you can stand with God. When you can't do anything, depend on His grace and strength to get you through. He gives you strength when you don't believe you can take one more step in your own strength.

3. <u>God's Power</u>—God's own power, the same power that created the universe and raised Jesus from the dead, is available to you and operative in you! Today! Take a look at the last line in our scripture, "the power of Christ rest upon me." That's HIS power working in YOU!

When we become insecure, we lose sight of all the rich and powerful promises God makes us in His word. Rest on these assurances!

- All things work together for good for you, child of God!
  Romans 8:28 KJV—"And we know that all things work together for good to them that love God, to them who are the called according to his purpose."
- He shall supply all your needs, child of God!
  Philippians 4:19 KJV—"But my God shall supply all your need according to his riches in glory by Christ Jesus."

- You can cast your cares on Him, because He cares for you, child of God!
  1 Peter 5:7 KJV—"Casting all your care upon him; for he careth for you."
- He doesn't turn on you, even when you mess up, because He is the same yesterday, today, and forever!
  Hebrews 13:8 KJV—"Jesus Christ the same yesterday, and today, and forever."
- You don't need anything He can't give you, because He is Jehovah Jireh, the God Who Provides!
  Genesis 22:14—"And Abraham called the name of the place, The-Lord-Will-Provide [Jehovah-Jireh]; as it is said to this day, 'In the Mount of the Lord it shall be provided.'"

When you struggle with pain, not only is He there with you but He is both able and willing to take your pain and sustain you with His grace, His strength, and His power.

Here we are again, at our bottom line. The bottom line is your insecurity can be made secure, but *only in Christ*! (Luke 23:41–43). You can't have security in this world, in your bank account, or relationships, but you can have security in Christ. Even though you may say all hope is gone, there is still hope! He did not create you only for this time, but for eternity.

Remember the thief on the cross, condemned with absolutely no hope. In his last moments, as he hung there helpless and hopeless, Jesus demonstrated His grace, His strength, and His power, along with his incredible and limitless love: "Today you will be with Me in paradise."

Do you crave the security of that grace, strength, power, and love? Look to the cross. Jesus says, as He did to the thief, "You will be with Me in paradise. Your insecurity will become secure, because of Me. Your name is written in My Father's book. You may go through hell here on earth, but no matter what you go through here, you can have security because you know Me and I know You, and because you know Me, you also know My Father" (Eph. 1:3–6).

He calls. Come. Bring your insecurities and lay them to rest at the foot of the cross. Cast your cares on Him, for He cares for you!

Conclusion

Pain. It is something we all experience. We have or will have physical pain, whether it is a paper cut or cancer, but we will also all suffer from mental or emotional pain. Where do you run to get away from your pain? I have stated several times that I do not have a magic cure for your pain. We all have different pain, and we all run from pain. Every time we run from something we run to something. What are you running to?

Are you running from everyone and everything and isolating yourself? Do you feel like Elijah in the cave hiding from Jezebel? Are you trying to find the answers in the destructive earthquake or fire? Is your pain so loud that you can't hear the still, small voice of God?

Are you flirting with disaster or have already found it in an inappropriate relationship? Are you like the adulteress woman afraid of being caught in your sin and having it dragged to the public square? Are you one of the accusers, the religious elite, who forgot you are the bride of Christ?

Are you the prodigal son who said "Give me my inheritance"? Do you think "you got this"? Is your theme song, "My Way"? Does your life smell like a pigsty? Are you suffering the worst kind of poverty, spiritual poverty?

What is important to you? Is it the best job or most money? Are you driven by the desire for the nicest house or coolest car? Have you traded the glory of God for cheap figurines? Who sits on the throne of your heart? You, your family, your friends, your stuff or the one who deserves it?

Are you one that runs to numbness? Have you felt the sting of intoxication? Have your eyes beheld "strange women"? Have you felt the seasickness of intoxication? Do you battle daily with your body's need for a poison?

Do you have all the answers? Do you have a degree in everything? Do you stand with your head up and think, "I'm glad I'm not like so-and-so"? Do you love for people to know how much you know?

Are you too stubborn for your own good? Do you see the Pharisee when you look in the mirror?

Do you feel worthless? Do you feel like Moses, who argued with God when called to help free the Israelites? Do you feel like Sarah, doubting your purpose and abilities? Are you the thief, hanging on the cross, no hope for a future?

When we run from something, we run to something, and God created us to run to Him. Jesus tells us, "These things I have spoken to you, that in Me you may have peace. In the world you will have tribulation; but be of good cheer, I have overcome the world" (John 16:33). He promises us peace! God knows your pain and understands better than anyone how to help you overcome it. It may be that God will work a miracle and take your pain completely away when you submit to Him, or He may choose to use your pain to shape and mold you into the person He created you to be. The point is He loves you and wants you to choose Him as your Pain Taker!

If you have questions about asking the Lord in your heart please contact us at www.jcimpact.org.

Dear Reader,

In preparation for this teaching series and sub-sequent book, I talked with so many people. I have come to realize that we don't have a pain-killer problem, we have a pain problem. I have said throughout, everyone's pain is different, but we all at one time experience physical, mental, or emo-tional pain. It is possible that you have experienced one or all these, and that is why you picked up this book. Maybe you are tired of running to all the wrong painkillers.

The Lord has moved in so many hearts with these messages. My prayer is that He has spoken to you also. If He has, and you would like more in-formation on this book, there more resources avail-able at our website, www.jcimpact.org.

If you have questions about how to start a re-lationship with Jesus you can go to our website, www.jcimpact.org.

In Christ's Love,

Rev. Jacky Connell

About The Author

Rev. Jacky Connell received the call to ministry at a young age. He became a pastor in 1981 and has served as senior pastor of Eden Westside Baptist Church for the past thirty years.

Reverend Connell has a passion for preaching and teaching the word of God. He believes that any individual can unlock his or her full potential through an empowering personal relationship with Jesus Christ.

Reverend Connell currently lives in Leeds, Alabama, with his wife. Together, they have two children and four grandchildren.